Another Drop of Irish Jokes

Published in 2005 for
Lagan Books

by
Appletree Press Ltd
The Old Potato Station
14 Howard Street South
Belfast, BT7 1AP

Tel: +44 (0) 28 90 24 30 74
Fax: + 44 (0) 28 90 24 67 56
E-mail: reception@appletree.ie
Web-site: www.appletree.ie

Design & Layout © Appletree Press Ltd, 2005

A catalogue record for this book is available from the British Library.

Another Drop of Irish Jokes

ISBN: 0 86281 983 0

Desk & Marketing Editor: Jean Brown
Editor: Jim Black
Design: Stuart Wilkinson
Production Manager: Paul McAvoy

9 8 7 6 5 4 3 2 1

AP3278

Dedicated to Irishmen and Irishwomen all over the world.

Another Drop of Irish Jokes

Terry Adlam

LAGAN BOOKS

Finnegan had died and his wife Mary invited everyone back to the house for the wake. Finnegan's brother was first back and saw that the front room was full of crates of stout, whiskey, lager, cider, beer and wine. On the table near the alcohol mountain was a plate with two slices of bread on it. When Mary entered the room Finnegan's brother asked:

'Mary, what's all the bread for?'

An Irishman was a bit the worse for drink at a party when he talked to the host.

'Excuse me, but do you know if lemons have legs and feathers?'

'Of course they don't!' said the host.

'Oh dear,' slurred the Irishman. 'I think I've just squeezed your canary into my gin and tonic.'

Three Irishmen were driving across the desert when their truck broke down.

'We're going to have to walk,' said the first one. 'We'd best take what we can from the truck to help us make it across the desert. I'll take this big bottle of water.'

'I'll take this bag of food,' said the second one.

'And I'll take this!' said the third Irishman, removing the driver's door.

'What on earth do you want to take that for?' asked the first.

'Well, when we're walking across the sand,' explained the third Irishman, 'and we get a bit hot, we could wind the window down to help cool us down.'

An Irishman went to see Riverdance when it toured Dublin. When he arrived at the theatre the clerk in the box-office asked:

'And where would you like to sit, Sir?'

'The shallow end.'

Two Irish girls are walking down the road when one of them notices a small compact on the pavement and picks it up. She opens it and looks into the mirror.

'I'm not sure who this belongs to, but her face looks very familiar.'

'Here, let me have a look.'
The second girl looks in the mirror. 'You eejit, it's me.'

'Oh it must be yours then!'

'It can't be!' says the second girl. 'I lost mine along this road some time last week.'

An Irishman went into a museum and accidentally knocked over a Ming vase. The museum curator went ballistic.

'Do you know that that vase you just knocked over was over a thousand years old?!' she screamed.

'Sure that oul thing,' smiled the Irishman. 'It's lucky it wasn't new.'

A blind tourist called Seymour walks into a pub in Dublin. He orders a drink.

'Who wants to hear some Irish jokes?' he shouts.

The whole pub goes quiet and then Seymour hears the barman's Irish accent.

'Before you tell any Irish jokes,' he growls, 'I think it's best to warn you that I'm Irish, and so is my barmaid, a black belt in karate. She lives with one the bouncers on the door, who is 6 foot 7, weighs 200lb and is a professional Irish wrestling champion. Also there are six big Irish rugby players sitting over in the corner. So think about this and ask yourself—do you really want to tell any Irish jokes in this pub?'

'No, not now,' says Seymour. 'Especially if I'm going to have to explain them all nine times.'

Did you hear about the fire in the Irish library?

Both the books were burnt, even the colouring-in ones!

An Irishman asked his wife what she would like for her birthday.

'Oh I'd love to be ten again!' she said wistfully.

So on her birthday before she could say anything, her husband whisked her off to a theme park. He took her on all the rides. He bought her candyfloss and afterwards took her to see a *Harry Potter* movie. After that he treated her to a burger dinner with the free toy and when they got home, he told his exhausted wife that she could stay up until nine o'clock as it was her birthday. Just before she went to bed he also made her some hot chocolate.

'Did you enjoy being 10 again?' he asked.

'I meant *size* 10!' his wife snapped.

An Irishman was showing his best friend around his new flat after a night out on the drink. His friend was curious about the big gong that stood in the middle of the living room.

'What's that?'

'It's my new speaking clock.'

'So how does it work?'

'I'll show you.'

The Irishman picked up the hammer and struck the gong with a resounding clang! Suddenly there was knocking from the other side of the wall followed by a very irate voice.

'Can you not hit that gong so loudly! Do you know it's a quarter past three in the morning!'

The Irishman's wife watches as he swipes flies in the living room.

'Killed any yet?'

'Five!' says he proudly. 'Three males and two females.'

'How could you tell what sex they were?'

'Easy,' says the Irishman. 'Three were on a beer can and two were on the phone.'

Another Drop of Irish Jokes

Mal met Cal at a local football match.

'How's the game going?'

'Great!' said Cal. 'It's end to end stuff.'

'Good match, then?'

'It is,' said Cal, 'and I think it's down to the managers and their motivational skills.'

'What do you mean?' asked Mal.

'Well the manager of the team in red has promised every man that scores a free bottle of stout. While the manager of the whites had promised every man who scores a bottle of best Irish whiskey.'

'That sounds interesting!' Mal said. 'What's the score at the moment?'

'72 all!' replied Cal.

'I put on a clean pair of pants and a clean pair of socks, every day,' an Irishman boasted to no one in particular. 'The only problem is, come the end of the month, I can't get me trousers and shoes on.'

Two Irishmen met one day.

'Hey, do you remember Ardel O'Flynn, from school?' said the first Irishman.

The second Irishman thought for a while.

'Yeah I remember O'Flynn, always came top of the class, went to Cambridge and got a doctorate in chemical engineering and a degree in medicine. He also toured the world and wrote a book, in Russian, on the political state of Eastern Europe.'

'That's the one. Well I met him the other day!'

'Really, what did you say to him?' the second Irishman asked.

'Do you want fries with that?'

Paddy and Thaddy were walking past a forest when they saw a sign that read:

'Wanted. Tree Fellers.'

'Oh that's a shame!' said Paddy. 'If Shamus had been with us, we could have applied for that job.'

The Irishman noticed that his little daughter had made a fire engine out of a pram, a garden hose and a little ladder. He also noticed that she had not only tied a rope from the toy engine to the collar of the family's pet dog, to help pull it along, but also another rope from the toy engine to the tail of the family cat.

'That's a lovely fire engine you've got there, but don't you think it would be better if you tied the rope round the cat's collar?'

'But Daddy, I wouldn't have a siren then!'

The Dublin building site manager wasn't one of Ireland's most compassionate men. One of his scaffolders arrived an hour late for work one morning all covered in bumps, bruises and blood. The manager asked what had happened.

'I fell down the stairs!'

'And that took you a whole hour?'

An Irishman had just spent a romantic night with his new girlfriend when he noticed a picture of a man on her mantlepiece.

'That's not your husband, is it?' he asked nervously.

'No, of course not,' she said.

'Is it your boyfriend?'

'No,' said the girl. 'You're my boyfriend now.'

'Is it a relative?'

'No.'

'Well who is it then?' the Irishman demanded.

'You are silly,' said the new girlfriend. 'It's me before the surgery.'

'Waiter!' called the Irishman as he sat in an expensive restaurant.

'Yes Sir?' replied the waiter.

'This soup is horrible. It has no taste, it's watery and it smells of lemon.'

'That's your finger bowl, Sir,' sniffed the waiter.

Two Irishmen knocked on the door of their local convent. The Mother Superior opened it and asked the Irishmen what they wanted.

'Excuse me, Mother Superior,' said one, 'but do you have any nuns here that are under three feet?'

The Mother Superior thought about it.

'No, we don't. If we did have a nun that small, I would surely know about it.'

'Oh thanks very much,' said the first Irishman in relieved tones.

'See? I told you it was a penguin we knocked down in the truck.'

Did you hear about the Irish girl who had to give up her cello lessons?

The cello was too heavy and it really hurt her neck when she put it under her chin!

The priest was giving a sermon on the evils of drink.

'…and if you continue to drink, you will gradually get smaller and smaller until you're the size of a mouse.'

When the Irishman got home he told his wife what the priest had said.

'So are you going to give up the drink?'

'No,' he replied. 'I'm going to kill the cat.'

A wife noticed her husband Thaddy leaning over the neighbour's fence. Every so often he would shout:

'Green side up!'

She watched for a while and her husband kept on shouting.

'Green side up! Green side up!'

'Thaddy,' she eventually called. 'What's going on?'

'It's Paddy, next door,' he called back. 'He's laying some new turf.'

An Irishman in America met two guys in a bar and had a few pints. One guy said that there was a building a few blocks away where, because of the strange wind thermal around it, one could jump off the building and float.

The Irishman said that he didn't believe it, but the two guys said they would show him.

'Watch!' said the first guy as they stood on the roof of the building. To the Irishman's amazement, the guy leapt off the building, floated for a few seconds and then landed back on the roof.

'That's amazing. Let me have a go!' said the Irishman as he leapt into the air... and fell 50 storeys to his death.

The guy who hadn't jumped off the building turned to the guy who had.

'You know, Superman, you're quite nasty after you've had a few drinks.'

An old Irishwoman went to her local newspaper and asked the girl on the desk how much was it to put a death notice in the paper, as her husband of 45 years had recently died.

'It's a pound a word,' said the girl.
So the old Irishwoman wrote on a piece of paper 'Bill is dead.'

'Is that all you want?' asked the girl.

'It's all I can afford,' said the old Irishwoman.
Feeling sorry for the old woman, the girl opened her purse and gave her three pounds.

'There, you can write a bit more now.'
The old Irishwoman thanked the girl and wrote on another piece of paper. 'Bill is dead. Lawnmower for sale.'

It was an Irishman's first day on the Cork building site and already things weren't going too well. The foreman really confused him–he showed him a selection of spades and told him to take his pick.

An Irishman was walking with his horse when a tourist rushed up to him.

'What a wonderful horse. How much?'

'I'm not selling him because he don't look too good,' said the Irishman.

'He looks wonderful!' the tourist replied. 'I'll give you £1000.'

'But he don't look too good,' repeated the Irishman.

'Rubbish, he looks great. How about £2000?'

He rubbed his head. 'I'm not sure.'

'OK,' said the tourist. 'Here's £10,000. It's yours if you let me buy your horse and ride away on it.'

'OK,' said the Irishman and next minute he was £10,000 richer and the tourist had mounted the horse and galloped off... straight into a tree.

The Irishman was standing over the tourist when he came round, and said.

'You didn't tell me that your horse was blind?!'

'Well,' said the Irishman, 'I did tell you that he didn't look too good.'

An Irishman was sitting in the lounge bar at Dublin Airport chatting to the barman.

'I've come to meet my brother,' he said. 'He's flying in from Australia and I haven't seen him for forty years.'

'That's nice,' said the Barman. 'Do you think you'll recognise him after all these years?'

'Probably not,' sighed the Irishman. 'After all, he has been away for a long time.'

'He probably won't recognise you either,' smiled the barman.

'Oh, of course he will! I haven't been away at all.'

An Irishman went to see his doctor.

'It's drink that's made you into the slovenly, drunken, incontinent, rude and violent person that you are.'

'Oh thanks Doc!' said the Irishman, greatly relieved. 'And the wife always said it was *my* fault.'

Another Drop of Irish Jokes

An Irishman was stuck in an Irish bog and sinking fast. Luckily his neighbour was passing by and offered to pull him out. Now although he is a strong man and the Irishman was a titchy little fella, the neighbour just couldn't pull the little Irishman out. He pulled and he heaved, but to no avail.

'I'm going into town to get some help,' said the neighbour.

'You can't do that!' screamed the Irishman. 'I'd have sunk by then.'

'Well, what else can we do?' asked the neighbour.

'You could try again and this time I'll take me feet out of the stirrups.'

So how many Irishmen does it take to change a light bulb?

Six—one to change the light bulb, two to get the drinks in and four to sing about how grand the old bulb was.

A priest walks into a pub and talks to the first Scotsman he meets.

'Do you want to go to heaven?'

'I do Father,' says the man.

'Good on you. Then go stand by the wall.' The priest then talks to an Englishman.

'Do you want to go to heaven?' The Englishman is quick to answer.

'Certainly, Father.'

'Good on you, too. Go stand by the wall.' Finally the priest comes up to an Irishman. When asked the same question, the Irishman says 'No'.

'I don't believe this!' exclaims the priest. 'You're saying that when you die you don't want to go to heaven?'

'Oh, when I die, I do,' says the Irishman. 'I thought you were getting a group together to go straight away.'

A tourist walks into a cocktail bar in Dublin, looks at what is on offer, then orders an 'Irish Cocktail.' He gets a pint of stout with a potato in it!

An Irishwoman was standing by a full-length mirror in her underwear, while her husband was in bed reading.

'Oh look at me. I'm fat. I'm going grey. My backside is enormous. My bust is saggy and every day I seem to get another wrinkle. I just feel I look oul and ugly.'

'I'll tell you something though,' said her husband, lowering his book.

'What's that?' asked the Irishwoman.

'There's nothing wrong with your eyesight.'

An Irishman was going up to the top deck of a bus when he spoke to the conductor.

'Can I bring up a crate of stout?'
The conductor thought for a bit.

'I don't see why not.'

'Thank you,' said the Irishman and promptly threw up over the stairs.

An Irishman goes into an electrical shop and speaks to one of the assistants.

'Excuse me, where do you keep the Potato Clocks?'

'I'm sorry, Sir,' said the assistant, 'you want what?'

'I want a Potato Clock,' insisted the Irishman.

'I'm afraid Sir, that there is no such thing as a Potato Clock.'

'There must be!' said the Irishman. 'My boss told me yesterday that I've got to get a Potato Clock, so that I can be at work by half past eight.'

An Irish girl was driving along the motorway when she got a call from her boyfriend.

'Be careful, because I've just heard on the radio that there is a car going the wrong way down the motorway you're on.'

'It's not just one car,' said the Irish girl. 'There's hundreds of them.'

An Englishman, a Scotsman and an Irishman wanted to get in to see the Dublin Olympics, but they didn't have tickets. The Englishman saw a nearby building site and had an idea. He stripped down to his vest and shorts, grabbed a piece of scaffolding and went up to the competitors' gate.

'Smith, the pole vault,' he said. The guard let him in.

The Scotsman did the same, only he picked up a sledgehammer and said, 'MacDonald, hammer thrower,' and he was let in.

The Irishman arrived at the gate covered in scratches, cuts and blood on account of the barbed wire he had wrapped around himself.

He hobbled up to the guard and said, 'O'Grady, fencing.'

While most Irish girls are very pretty, one of them certainly wasn't. When she went into a room, mice threw themselves on to traps. One day she went into the confessional box.

'Bless me, Father, for I have sinned.'

What is it, child?' asked the priest.

'Father, I have committed the sin of vanity!' bellowed the ugly Irish girl. 'I keeping looking in the mirror at home and telling myself how beautiful I am.'

The priest turned and looked at her.

'My child, I have good news. That isn't a sin - it's a mistake.'

The doctor rang up the old Irish gent to see if the pills he had prescribed a couple of weeks ago had improved his strength.

'Not very well,' wheezed the old Irish gent. 'I can't get the lid off the bottle.'

Two Irish hunters had gone to America to hunt bear. While they were driving through what they were told was 'Bear Country', they came to a fork in the road.

'Would you look at that!' said one of the Irishmen pointing to a road sign that read BEAR LEFT.

'We're too late.'

An Irish girl was working as a waitress in a Dublin restaurant when a fat fussy tourist called her over. He was holding up a piece of pork with a fork.

'Waitress,' he sneered, 'look at this, does it look like a pig to you.'

'Which end of the fork are we talking about, Sir?' the Irish girl sweetly smiled.

An Irishman and his wife returned home early and could hear their son in the living room about to propose to his girlfriend. The Irishman's wife didn't want to be accused of eavesdropping and spoiling the moment.

'Should we cough and let them know we can hear them?'

'Cough? Why should I cough?' said the Irishman. 'Nobody coughed to warn me when I proposed to you.'

Three Irishmen walked out of the pub one lunchtime, into a windy street.

'Bejabers, it's windy," said one.

'No it's not!' replied the second. 'It's Thursday.'

'So am I,' said the third man. 'Let's go and have another drink.'

Up till now Nolan and Dolan had never left their very remote southern village. They were taking their first ever train ride up the west coast of Ireland. An attendant pushing a refreshment trolley arrived and asked the boys if they would like something.

'What's that bent yellow thing?' asked Nolan.

'I don't know,' said Dolan.

'It's a banana, Sir,' said the attendant. Having never seen or tasted a banana before, the two boys bought one each. Nolan had just bit into his as the train went into a tunnel. When it emerged, Nolan threw the banana away.

'I wouldn't eat that banana if I was you,' he said to Dolan. 'I took one bite and I went blind there for a couple of seconds.'

You can always spot the Irishman on the North Sea Oil Rigs. He's the one throwing bread to the helicopters.

29

An Irish girl saw her Dublin boss standing near the office shredder looking bemused. She asked if she could help.

'Yes,' said the Dublin boss. 'This is a very important report. Do you know how this thing works?'
The Irish girl turns on the machine, takes the report from her boss and proudly feeds it into machine.

'Oh that's brilliant! Thank you. I just need two copies.'

Did you hear about the unlucky Irishman?

He was crossing the road when a car hit him and knocked him thirty feet in the air, over a hedge and into a field. The police charged him with leaving the scene of an accident!

Ireland was due to meet Scotland in a big international rugby match so the Manager of the Irish team decided to get in some extra training. He rang up Madam Tussaud's in London and asked if he could borrow the waxworks of the Scottish team, so that the Irish lads could practice some moves. The waxworks were delivered to Lansdowne Road and training began. A couple of days later, an official from the Irish Rugby Board rang up to see how things were going.

'Not too good,' said the Manager. 'We had a practice match yesterday. Scotland won 16-4.'

An Irishman was walking through a back street in London when a mugger armed with a gun stepped out in front of him.

'Right, you!' he spat. 'Your money or your life?'

'You'll have to shoot me,' said the Irishman. 'I'm saving up for me old age.'

Pat was curious when he saw Mick pouring some of his best Irish whiskey onto his lawn.

'What you doing, Mick?'

'Saving time and energy,' said Mick.
Pat didn't understand.

'You know what a chore mowing the lawn is? Well, this is the best way to avoid cutting your grass. Just pour Irish whiskey on it.'

'How can that save you time and energy?' asked a still confused Pat.

'Well,' said Mick, 'the grass comes up half-cut already'.

An American went into a Dublin bar and thought he'd wind the barman up.

'Hey buddy, got any of them Helicopter Chips?'

The barman replied without a second thought.

'Sorry, Sir, we only do plain.'

Paddy rang Thaddy up to tell him about the trouble he was having with a jigsaw.

'It's very difficult,' said Paddy. 'There's loads of pieces, but I just can't seem to get them to join together and make the same picture of the tiger that's on the box.'

Thaddy told him not to worry and that he would be round soon to help.

When Thaddy arrived he saw Paddy sitting at a table trying to do his jigsaw. Thaddy looked at the pieces and looked at the box.

'Paddy, put the Frosties back in the box.'

Did you hear about the very unsuccessful Irish firing squad that used to stand in a circle?

When they finally decided that that formation didn't work, they tried lining up one behind the other!

An Englishman had always wanted to be an American and his doctor told him that there was an operation that he could undergo to remove 40% of his brain, which would leave him thinking and talking like an American. The man agreed. During the operation the doctor made a terrible mistake and waited until the man came round to tell him.

'Look,' he said when the man was awake, 'by accident, instead of 40% of your brain, I removed 75%.'

'Well bejabers,' said the man, 'you're not to be worrying too much about that, so you are.'

An Irish lad called Paddy and a Scots lad called Jock, were in the army and they were being made to march round the drill square in double quick time. The breathless Scot said to the Irishman.

'Aye, Paddy, I no like 'doubling'.'

'Well Jock, I'm not that keen on Edinburgh.'

An Irishman had married into money, but the marriage wasn't a happy one.

'If it wasn't for my money, this big house and all the things inside it like the TV and cinema room, the gym, the games room, the antique furniture, the state of the art sound system and the indoor swimming pool,' his wife shouted, 'wouldn't be here!'

'If it wasn't for your money,' the Irishman shouted back, '*I* wouldn't be here!'

Two Irish friends were going camping in Africa.

'I'm taking four bottles of whiskey with us, just in case we get bitten by a snake. What are you taking?'

'Some snakes!'

An Irishman went into his local college and asked if he could enrol in a night course in Japanese. He was given a registration form to fill in.

'I hope you don't mind me asking?' said the registration clerk. 'Why on earth do you want to study Japanese? It's such a hard language to master.'

'I know,' said the Irishman. 'But me and the wife have just adopted a Japanese baby and we want to be able to understand him when he starts to talk.'

An Irishman went into a timber yard.

'I'd like some planks of wood please.'

'What size?' asked the assistant.

'4 by 2 please.'

'Fine,' replied the assistant. 'And how long do you need them?'

'Well I'm building a house,' said the Irishman, 'so I'd like to keep them if possible.'

It was late at night and an Irish couple were asleep in bed when the bedside phone rang.

'Hello?' said the sleepy husband. 'What? How would I know, I'm a bus driver, not a weather man.'

'What was that about?' asked his wife as she was woken up by her husband slamming the phone down.

'Some eejit of a fella wanted to know if the coast was clear.'

A little Irish girl was in her back garden filling in a large hole.

'What're you doing?' asked her neighbour who was watching over the garden fence.

'My pet goldfish has died, so I'm burying him.'

'Oh dear!' said the neighbour. 'But that's a very big hole for a little goldfish.'

'I know,' said the little Irish girl, 'but that's because he's inside your cat.'

The Irish lady was eating an evening meal with her husband.

'When we were first married, you always insisted on me having the biggest portions. You used to always make sure I had the biggest piece of steak. You don't do that any more. Is it because you don't love me anymore?'

'Don't be silly darling. It's just that you cook so much better than when we were first married.'

An Irishwoman was taking her first plane ride and was curious when the stewardess offered her a hard boiled sweet.

'It's to keep your ears from popping at high altitudes,' she explained nicely.
At the end of the flight as the Irishwoman was getting off, the stewardess asked her if the sweets had worked.

'Not really,' said the Irishwoman, 'they kept falling out.'

An Irishman carrying a large salmon under his arm walks into his local fish and chip shop.

'Excuse me, but do you sell fishcakes?'

'We do, but unfortunately we've run right out,' the owner apologises.

'Oh that's a shame,' says the Irishman, nodding to the salmon under his arm. 'It's his birthday today.'

An Irishman was in the pub one night, boasting to everyone that he could name the capitals of all the world's countries. Of course no one believed him, but he insisted.

'OK brain-box, what's the capital of Venezuela?' asked the barman.

'That's easy,' said the Irishman. 'V!'

An Irishwoman was tired of being embarrassed when her husband referred to her as 'Mother of Six'. They were at a party recently and he called in a loud voice,

'Time to go home, 'Mother of Six'!'

The Irishwoman replied in an equally loud voice, 'Coming, 'Father of Four'!'

A man with a crocodile on a lead went into a pub in Wicklow and asked the barmaid.

'Excuse me miss, do you serve Irishmen?'

'Of course we do.'

'Great!' said the man. 'I'll have a pint, and an Irishman for my crocodile, please.'

An Irish lady went to see Dr Flynn D. Form, and told him of her problem.

'I keep thinking I'm cartoon characters,' she said. 'One day I think I'm Mickey Mouse, the next day I think I'm Donald Duck. This morning I woke up and thought I was Bambi.'

'That's very interesting,' said Dr Form, 'but nothing to worry about. You're just having some Disney spells.'

Frank O' Funnell was an underwater engineer for the Irish Marine Company. One day he was working under the Irish Sea from a boat up on the surface, when he received a message over the radio.

'Frank,' said the voice. 'This is Finnegan on the boat. Don't bother coming up.'

'Why?' asked Frank.

'We're sinking,' said Finnegan, 'so we'll come down to you.'

Did you hear the one about the Irish photographer who kept all his broken light bulbs?

He needed them for his dark room!

An Irishman went into a dirty English pub and was surprised to see a pig on the counter.

'Excuse me Sir,' asked the Irishman, 'but why is that pig on the bar?'

'What pig, mate?' the barman belched. The Irishman pointed to the porker draped across the counter.

'That's an air freshener.'

It was the Irishman's first day on the building site. He asked the foreman if he could hang his coat up in a nearby shed.

'That's not a shed,' said the foreman. 'That's your hod.'

An Irishman was on a skiing holiday in Switzerland. He went into a ski shop and asked the assistant,

'Tell me Sir, when I'm skiing down the hill, do I zig-zag or zag-zig?'

'I don't really know,' said the assistant. 'I'm a tobogganist.'

'Oh in that case,' said the Irishman, 'I'll have a packet of cigarettes and a box of matches, please.'

An Irishman was in East London and decided to visit a typical English nightclub. On the door, two big bouncers frisked him for weapons. When they found out he didn't have any, they gave him some.

An Irishman walked into a bar with a parrot on his head.

'Where on earth did you get that?' asked the barman. The parrot replied:

'Well, it started off as a little wart on my bum.'

Two Irishmen were out in a boat, fishing, when the boat sprung a leak.

'The boat's taking on water. What're we going to do?'

'Don't worry! I've made another hole down this end to let it out.'

Michael O'Shuaneghessymacker was Ireland's worst Grand Prix driver. In the Monte Carlo Grand Prix he made 100 pit stops— once to fill up with fuel, the other 99 times to ask for directions.

The Irish builder had spent six weeks building a 60 foot tall chimney in the middle of one of Farmer O'Toole's fields.

'There's it finished,' the Irish builder said as he showed the farmer. 'But why do you want a chimney in the middle of the field?'

'I don't!' Farmer O'Toole fumed. 'You've had the plans upside down. I wanted a well.'

Paddy didn't seem his usual self when Thaddy met him for a drink one night.

'What's up?' Thaddy asked.

'Oh I don't know,' sighed Paddy. 'I keep getting these spots before my eyes.'

'Really?' asked Thaddy. 'Have you seen a doctor?'

'No,' replied Paddy, 'only spots.'

Did you hear the one about the Irish girl who spent all her money on a trip to Warsaw?

She wanted to be a Pole dancer!

The widow of a rich Irish man sat expectantly in the solicitor's office for the reading of his will. The solicitor opened the letter and began to read.

'I, Patrick James Connelly being of sound mind...spent all my money before I died.'

An Irish couple were parked in a secluded spot on Lovers' Lane.

'Do you want to get into the back seat?' he whispered in his girlfriend's ear.

'No, I want to stay in the front with you.'

An Irish girl was going to go to New York on her holidays and wanted to know how much time the journey would take.

'How long is the flight from Dublin to New York?' asked the Irish girl, when she rang the airline company.

'Just a minute,' said the operator.

'That quick?' replied the Irish girl.

Did you hear about the Irishman who travelled all the way to Dublin to change his name to AIG 2065 just so he could have a personalised car registration number plate?

No one is saying that she was a bit thick, but she was the only Irish woman I know who would smile during a lightning storm, convinced someone was taking her photograph.

Scientists have discovered a rare, native Irish butterfly in the Cork countryside. They know that the beautifully marked butterfly is Irish, because after a while it turns into a caterpillar.

Irish people are brilliant at languages. They can understand many tongues such as French, German, Italian, Russian and Swahili... as long as they're spoken in Irish.

A while ago there was talk of an Irish Mafia being set up in Belfast. It didn't last long because the Godfather Don O'Killarney kept making offers he couldn't remember or understand.

Irish stuntman Derval O'Knievel was badly injured a couple of weeks back when a stunt he was performing went wrong. He was trying to jump twenty-five motorbikes in a bus.

Did you hear the one about the Tug of War contest between Dublin and Cork?

It was cancelled because they couldn't find a long enough rope!

Of course you all know why Irishmen go around it threes? You don't?

Well let me explain—it's because one of them can usually read, one can usually write and the third likes to hang about with intellectuals.

The captain of a Spanish galleon looked through his telescope.

'Pirates ahoy!' shouted the captain. 'Off the starboard side, and the captain is an Irishman.'

'Excuse me captain,' said the First Mate who was standing nearby. 'How do you know that the pirate captain is an Irishman?'

'Easy, First Mate,' answered the captain. 'He's the only pirate wearing a patch over each eye.'

One night an Irishman brought home a pig from the pub.

'You're not bringing that thing in this house,' screamed his wife.

'Why not?' slurred the Irishman.

'Because of the smell!' she shrieked.
The Irishman burped.

'Oh don't worry about that, I'm sure he'll get used to it after a while.'

O'Knowe goes onto an Irish quiz show.

'What is fourteen plus fourteen?'

After a pause, O'Knowe says, 'Nineteen!'

The audience, made up of O'Knowe's friends and family and other Irish people, shouts out,

'Give him another chance! Give him another chance!'

The quiz-master smiles and asks another question.

'What is five plus five?'

After even longer than the last time O'Knowe says, 'Forty-six.'

The quiz-master shakes his head as the audience once again began to chant.

'Give him another chance! Give him another chance!'

Just before the quiz-master is about to ask the third question, he whispers to O'Knowe:

'The next answer is four, OK?'

The quiz-master ask him what two plus two is and quick as a shot O'Knowe says, 'FOUR!'

The audience go mad chanting:

'Give him another chance! Give him another chance!'

An Irishman was hiking across America and got a lift from an American husband and wife driving a pick-up truck. There wasn't a lot of room in the front, so the Irishman sat in the back of the truck. While driving across a bridge, the husband lost control of the pick-up and it fell over the side of the bridge into a river. After the pick-up had sunk, the husband and wife fought their way out of the cab and surfaced. A couple of minutes later the Irishman came out of the water, gasping for air.

'Where have you been?' the wife called.

'I couldn't get the tailgate open,' spluttered the Irishman.

Big Brenda O'Nasty goes to her doctor to find out why she is feeling so unwell.

'Your problem Miss O'Nasty, is that you are too fat,' says the doctor.

Brenda isn't impressed.

'I'd like a second opinion, if you don't mind.'

'OK,' replies the doctor, 'you're ugly as well.'

An Irish girl asked her doctor to recommend a diet.

'The most effective diet I know,' said the doctor, 'is the one where you eat anything you want for the first two days of your diet. Then skip the third day and then start again.'

The Irish girl did as the doctor had said. She went home and ate anything she wanted for the first two days, then she skipped the third day. Then she ate anything she wanted for the next two days, and then she skipped the third day after that. This went on for about three weeks and then she went back to see the doctor.

'So how's your diet going?'

'Not too bad,' said the Irish girl. 'The first two days are OK, but all that skipping on the third day really tires me out.'

A man was going to have new revolutionary brain transplant operation. The brain surgeon was showing him the brains he could choose from and how much they would cost.

'Well, here we have the brain of an Englishman and that's £1000. Then we have the brain of a Scotsman, which is £5000 and then there is the brain of an Irishman which would cost you £1,000,000.'

'Why is the Irishman's brain so expensive?' asked the man.

'Because it's hardly ever been used.'

The Irish boy had a feeling that his mother didn't like him when she used to give him his school packed lunch wrapped in a map.

As if that wasn't bad enough, when he came home from school, his mother used to send him out to steal hubcaps off moving cars.

'Any last requests?' sneered the captain of the Mexican firing squad as Paddy stood against the wall. 'A blindfold? A cigarette maybe?'

'No,' said Paddy. 'I'd like to sing a song.'

'Very well, you sing your song, Irishman, then we shoot you.'

Paddy took a deep breath and began singing.

'40 million green bottles hanging on the wall, 40 million green bottles hanging on the wall...'

'I feel like being romantic tonight,' sighed the Irishwoman. 'Why don't you take me out for an expensive meal at an exclusive restaurant, where we can eat exotic food and drink vintage champagne? After that we can kiss and dance the night away. Why I might even let you drink champagne out of my shoe.'

'Now, that's a kind offer,' said her husband, 'but I don't think I could manage 8 pints of champagne in one night.'

An Irish student was telling his friend how he had password-protected his computer.

'And what's your password?'

'Well, don't tell anybody,' says the Irish student 'but it's "James Bond, Indiana Jones, Superman, Spider-man, Shrek, Harry Potter".'

'What made you choose a password like that?' his friend asked.

'Because,' said the Irish student, 'I was told that it had to have at least six characters.'

A young Irish lad comes home from school one day and tells his Dad that he's got a part in the school play.

'That's great son,' says his Dad. 'What part are you playing?'

'I'm a husband of an Irishwoman.'

'That's no good son,' his Dad replies. 'Go back and tell your teacher you want a speaking role.'

The Irish detective arrived home from work looking very down.

'What's the matter?' asked his wife.

'I've been kicked out of the Serious Crime Squad.'

'Why?'

'I kept laughing.'

'Do you know it takes three sheep to make a cardigan?' said the Irish girl to her friend.

'Really?' replied the second Irish girl. 'That's amazing! I didn't even know that sheep could knit.'

An Irishman had locked his keys in his car and spent hours bending and fiddling with a coat hanger just trying to get the door open so that he could let his family out.

An Irishman was playing cricket when he was given out for a very dubious LBW. On the way back to the pavilion, he went up to the man in the white coat.

'That was never LBW. I was never out. You only called it because I'm Irish and you think I'm too thick to know any better. We're not a race of idiots you know.'

'It's got nothing to do with me,' said the man. 'I'm just selling ice creams.'

An Irishman driving in his car was stopped by the police one night just outside Kilkenny.

'Excuse me, Sir,' said the policeman. 'Do you know you're driving without a rear light?'

The Irishman got out of his car, looked and then broke down into floods of tears. The policeman was obviously concerned.

'Now come on, Sir,' he said. 'It's not such a serious offence. There's no need to get that upset.'

'Isn't there?' sobbed the Irishman. 'Well, you tell me what's happened to my caravan?'

An Irishman is in a rich neighbourhood touting for work as a handyman when he approaches a big house. He knocks on the door and asks the man if he wants any jobs doing for £50?

The man thinks for a while, then tells him that his porch round the side of the house needs painting. Could he do that for £50? The Irishman says he can.

The man tells the Irishman that all he needs is in the garden shed and to get on with it. In less than half an hour the Irishman is knocking on the front door again.

'Finished Sir!' he beams. 'I had enough paint to give it two coats.'

'Great,' says the man, complimenting the Irishman on his speed.

'All in a day's work, Sir,' says the Irishman. 'By the way, Sir, it's not a Porch, it's a Ferrari.'

An Irishman found a magic lamp and a genie willing to grant him three wishes. For his first wish the Irishman wished for a billion pounds in his Post Office savings account. The genie clapped his hands and the Irishman was now a billionaire.

Next the Irishman wished for a fleet of expensive cars. The genie clapped his hands and the Irishman was the proud owner of some Aston Martins, Porsches and Ferraris.

The Irishman's final wish was to be made irresistible to women. The genie clapped his hands and the Irishman changed into a box of chocolates.

Did you hear the one about the Irishman who was pleased when he got a 'Parking Fine' notice on his car window?

He thought the traffic warden was giving him a compliment!

An Irishman was accused of being the second in command of a big bank robbery.

'I wasn't second in command,' the Irishman told the judge. 'I was the mastermind.'

The Judge gave him two months for perjury.

An Irishwoman had bought a toilet brush and asked her husband to use it when he'd been to the toilet. A couple of days passed and the Irishwoman asked her husband if he had been using it.

'I have,' said the Irishman, 'but I prefer the toilet paper.'

Ireland's oldest inhabitant, Mrs Ann Chent, was celebrating her birthday and gave an interview to a local newspaper reporter.

'So why do you think you've lived to 110?'

'I guess it's because I was born such a long time ago,' said Ann.

An Irishman was being interviewed for a job on a Dublin building site.

'Can you make a decent cup of tea?' asked the foreman.

'I certainly can,' replied the Irishman.

'Good,' said the foreman. 'Can you drive a fork lift truck?'

'Why?' answered the Irishman. 'How big is the teapot?'

Did you hear about the Irishman who suggested to his mother-in-law that she take a holiday?

He told her to go to the Thousand Islands...and spend a week on each island!

English scientists had dug 50 metres underground in Kent and discovered small strips of copper. After studying the copper, they announced that the ancient Britons of 25,000 years ago had a nation-wide telephone network.

Hearing this the French decided to dig 100 metres underground in the Massif Central and found small pieces of glass. They studied the glass and announced that the ancient French of 55,000 years ago had a nation-wide fibre-optic telephone network.

The Irish then dug 200 metres down in the wilds of Killkenny and found absolutely nothing. They announced that the ancient Irish of 55,000 years ago had mobile phones.

An Irishman went up to the ticket office at Waterloo station in London.

'I want to go to Paris.'

'Eurostar?' asked the ticket salesperson.

'Well I sing a bit, but I'm no Daniel O'Donnell.'

An Irishwoman was sitting at her husband's bedside after some major surgery and he was starting to recover from the anaesthesia. His eyes started to open, he saw her and quietly spoke.

'Oh, you're beautiful.' Then he drifted back to sleep.

Later he woke again.

'Oh, you're cute.'

'What happened to "beautiful"?' his wife smiled at him.

'The drugs are wearing off,' he replied.

'Now Paddy, be honest with me,' his wife asked. 'If you didn't know, how old would you think I am?'

Paddy looked at her for a minute.

'Well looking at your skin, I'd say twenty, your hair, nineteen and your figure, twenty-five.'

'Oh Paddy,' beamed his wife, 'you are a flatterer.'

'Hang on,' Paddy said. 'I haven't added them up yet.'

An Irishwoman was woken up one night by her husband, sitting at the foot of the bed crying.

'What's wrong?' she asked.
Her husband looked up at her through tear drenched eyes.

'Remember, 25 years ago, when I got you pregnant? And your dad gave me the choice of either marrying you or going to jail?'

'Of course I remember!' replied his wife sympathetically.

'Well,' sobbed the Irishman, 'I would have been released tomorrow.'

A hiker on holiday in Ireland saw a local Irishman getting into his car.

''Scuse me mate,' asked the hiker. 'Can you give me a lift?'

'Sure,' said the Irishman. 'That's a nice suit your wearing, you're looking good. The world is yours for the taking. I like your smile…'

An eighty year old Irish woman made medical history when she gave birth to a baby girl. When she returned home her relatives came round to see her and the new arrival.

'Can we see the baby, mum?' her daughter asked.

'Not yet,' says the old lady. 'We have to wait until she cries.'

'Why?' asked her daughter.

'Because I forgot where I put her.'

An Irishman went up to customer services at his local supermarket.

'Excuse me,' he said to the lady on duty. 'I want to make a complaint. This vinegar I bought from here only this morning has got lumps in it.'

The woman looked at the bottle.

'Those are pickled onions, Sir.'

An Irishman walks into a job centre in Dublin.

'I'd like a job please.'

'Oh you might be in luck today,' says the woman behind the counter. 'There's a model who is also a millionairess who has just inherited a brewery who is looking for someone who can sample the beer and take her out partying most nights of the week in her Ferrari. She will pay £1000 a day and can offer 3 months holidays.'

The Irishman is amazed, but sceptical. 'You've got to be winding me up, so you have?'

'Well,' said the woman, 'you started it.'

'I hear Shamus was thrown out of Dublin Zoo the other day,' Paddy told Pat.

'Why?'

'He was feeding the penguins.'

'That's a wee bit harsh to throw him out for just doing that, don't you think?' replied Pat.

'Not really. He was feeding them to the lions!'

67

Farmer O'Dingle and Farmer O' Dell were out hunting when a hang glider flew over them.

'What's that great big thing up there?' said Farmer O'Dingle.

'It looks like a giant bird. Quick, shoot it!' suggested Farmer O'Dell.

Farmer O'Dingle took aim with his shotgun and fired.

'Did you get it?' asked Farmer O'Dell.

'I don't think so,' said Farmer O'Dingle. 'But at least it's let go of the little fella it was holding.'

An old Irishman went to see his doctor.

'Doctor every morning round about six o'clock I have to have a wee.'

'Well at your age, that's quite normal,' said the doctor.

'But Doc,' replied the old Irishman, 'I don't wake up until eight o'clock!'

An Irishman's ambition to be the first man from Ireland to sail single-handed around the world was in tatters last night when the Irish Yachting Association discovered he had used two hands and disqualified him for cheating.

A tourist went into a Dublin dress shop.

'Can I try on the lovely dress you've got in the window?'

'You can if you want, madam,' the assistant said, 'but in Ireland we prefer our customers to use the changing rooms.'

The Irishman's barbecue wasn't the success he thought it would be. The chicken, steaks, sausages and burgers were cooked to perfection, but the beans kept falling through the grill!

A Welshman, a Scot and an Englishman are standing on the bank of a very wide river that they must cross when the Welshman finds a magic lamp. He rubs it and a genie pops out and gives them each a wish.

'I wish I was 10% smarter so I could get across this river.'

Suddenly the Welshman turns into a powerful French swimmer and swims the river.

The Scot sees what happens and makes his wish.

'I wish I was 25% smarter so that I could get across this river.'

Suddenly the Scot turns into a German, builds a raft from trees and sails across the river.

Finally, the Englishman makes his wish.

'I wish I was 50% smarter so I could get across this river.'

Suddenly the Englishman turns into an Irishman and walks across the bridge.

One night an Irishman was walking home when four muggers jumped on him. The Irishman put up a fight but the muggers got the better of him. Finally three held him down while the fourth went through his pockets. All the mugger could find was 55p.

'55p?' the mugger exclaimed. 'You put up that fight for 55p. Why bother?'

'Oh is that all you wanted?' said the Irishman. 'I thought you were after the £500 I've got hidden in my shoes.'

'Betty?' asked Tom. 'It's such a glorious day, is it not? What do you think the neighbours would say if I mowed the lawn in just my shorts?'

'Probably that I married you for your money,' sighed Betty.

71

An Irishman went to heaven and arrived at the Pearly Gates. St Peter checked his name on the booking-in sheet.

'It doesn't look like we've got you booked in for today. Tell me, what was your occupation when you were alive?'

'I had my own business. I was a scrap metal merchant,' the Irishman informed St Peter.

'I just need to check something,' said St Peter. 'I'll be back in a minute.' And off he went. When he returned the Irishman had gone, and so had the Pearly Gates.

Paddy was looking at Thaddy's new dog.

'Thaddy? Your dog hasn't got a tail.'

'I know,' replied Thaddy.

'Well how do you know when it's happy?' asked Paddy.

'It stops biting me,' Thaddy sighed.

Did anybody hear about the time a few years ago when in Belfast City Hall, the Irish Philharmonic Orchestra was playing 'The Bermuda Rhapsody' and the triangle player disappeared?

An Irishman had got a job on the door of a Dublin nightclub. One night a clubber came up to him and asked if he could take a pair of jump leads into the club. The Irishman thought for a while.

'Well, OK, but just don't start anything.'

'Mammy,' called the little Irish girl as she came running in to the kitchen. 'There's a man with a bill at the front door.'

'Don't be silly,' said her Mammy. 'It must be a duck with a hat on.'

'Have we any news on that Irish woman they found drowned in her shower?' asked the detective.

'Yes Sir,' said the sergeant. 'She died through washing her hair continuously for a week.'

The detective was amazed.

'Apparently she was just following instructions,' the sergeant replied, handing the detective the empty shampoo bottle on which was written:

1. Wet hair
2. Apply shampoo
3. Wait 3 minutes
4. Rinse
5. Repeat

'I've been married for thirty years,' an Irishman told his pal, 'and do you know, I'm still in love with the same woman.'

'That's nice,' said his pal.

'I know, but if me wife finds out, I'm in trouble.'

Another Drop of Irish Jokes

An Irishman brought a piece of M.F.I. self-assembly furniture and he had it constructed and ready in a matter of minutes. It wasn't difficult. The diagrams were easy to follow and the final cabinet looked just like it did in the big picture on the front of the box.

It was so simple to do, a child could do it; which just goes to prove that M.F.I. stands for 'Made For Irishmen!'

An Irish boy went up to the ice cream van.

'Would you like a flake in that?' asked the ice cream man.

'Yes please!' smiled the Irish boy.

'Would you like hundreds and thousands?' the ice cream man asked again.

'No, just the one please,' said the Irish boy. 'Me mammy doesn't like me to have too much chocolate.'

'My wife told me last night that she suffers from Marital Thrombosis!' Dan told Van.

'Marital Thrombosis?' repeated Van. 'What's that?'

'I'm not sure,' said Dan, 'but the wife said she's got it because she married a clot.'

A boy had been 'chatting up' a lovely Irish lass all evening at the nightclub. It was going so well until he asked if he could see her home and she showed him a photo of her parents' house.

Did you hear about the Irishman who went to Amsterdam?

He stood outside all night waiting for the Red Lights to change!

A young Irish lass went to a hairdresser's one day, listening to a mp3 player through a set of headphones. She told the hairdresser what she wanted, but also mentioned that her headphones must not be removed. The hairdresser tried her best, but while she was brushing the lass's hair, she accidentally knocked the headphones off. Almost immediately the Irish lass went blue, collapsed and fell on the floor. The hairdresser was both shocked and very confused. She picked up the headphones and was about to put them back on when she could hear something coming from them, that wasn't music. She held the headphones closer to her ear and heard:

'Breathe in... Breathe out...Breathe in... Breathe out...'

Did you hear about the Irish girl who spent a whole day in her local library?

She was studying for a blood test!

'Paddy,' called his mammy, 'why haven't you changed the water in the goldfish tank?'
'Because,' replied Paddy, 'they haven't finished drinking what they got last week.'

Two Irishmen were walking along a road.
'Hey look at that dead bird.'
The second Irishman looked up in the sky.
'Where?'

'Well what do you think of it?' asked the Englishman, who was showing Stonehenge to his Irish visitor.

'It'll be nice when it's finished,' said the Irishman.

Did you hear about the Irish woman who told her husband she would like to celebrate her birthday in something long and flowing?

He threw her in the river!

I'm not saying that he was the laziest man in Ireland, but he spent three weeks off work on the building site with a broken thermos flask.

I'm not saying that O'Flynn was lazy, but it had been such a long time since he last cut the grass in his back garden, his wife had to hang her washing out on horseback.

Did you hear the story about the Irish snob?

She refused to travel in the same car as her chauffeur!

Did you hear the one about the thin Irishman?

He was so thin that when he walked past the snooker table, somebody tried to chalk his head!

An Irishman rang up his council to complain about the big puddle he had in his back garden and asked them to do something about it. A day later they sent him three ducks.

Did you hear the one about the Irish scientist working for the fashion industry who crossed a mink with a gorilla?

He got a beautiful fur coat but the arms were too long!

An Irishman phoned the doctor.

'Doc, I need some more of those sleeping pills for my wife.'

'Why, has she run out of them?' asked the doctor.

'No,' said the Irishman, 'she's woken up!'

An Irishman went into a pub.
'A pint of less, please.'
'What's Less?' asked a puzzled barman.
'No idea,' replied the Irishman. 'But my doctor says I've got to start drinking it.'

An Irishman goes into a flag shop in Dublin and asks,
'What colour are your Irish flags?'
'Green, White and Orange,' says the shopkeeper, surprised.
'Ok' says the Irishman. 'I'll have a green one please.'

An Irishman went into a bar and ordered 4 bitters, two red wines, one white wine, two whiskeys, a gin and tonic, a coke and four packets of cheese and onion crisps.
The barman made up the order.
'Do you want a tray?'
'No thanks,' said the Irishman. 'I've got enough to carry as it is.'

An Irishman was moaning about the amount of overtime he has to work, to his wife one evening.

'Sure I'll be coming in so late one night, I'll meet myself going out to work.'

An Irishman went to his doctor.

'Doc, I've go' a problem. I ca' pro'ou'ce my Ts, my Fs and my Ns.'

'Well you can't say fairer than that then,' replied the doctor.

'Two pints of beer and an orange please,' asked the Irishman up at the bar.

'Still orange?' enquired the barman.

'Oh yes,' said the Irishman.
'She hasn't changed her mind.'

83

'Where's the telly gone?' called the Irishman when he walked into the pub.

'Someone broke in last night and stole it,' the landlord told him.

'Well I'm not that surprised,' said the Irishman. 'You did stick it in the corner where everyone could see it.'

Two Irishmen were walking home along some railway tracks.

'There's an awful a lot of steps here.'

'You're telling me,' said second Irishman. 'But I'll tell you what's worse; this handrail is very low.'

An Irishwoman goes to see her doctor.

'Doctor, my husband keeps washing his car.'

'That's not unusual. Most men wash their cars,' said the doctor.

'In the bath?' she sighed.

'Hey Paddy!' called Thaddy from across the garden fence. 'Are you going fishing, today?'

'Yes I am!' replied Paddy.

'Have you got worms?' asked Thaddy.

'Yeah,' answered Paddy, 'but the doctor said I could still go fishing.'

'So how's the new job?' an Irish grandpa asked his grandson.

'I'm a Monback,' replied the young man. The grandpa looked confused. 'A Monback? What's a Monback?'

'I work in a delivery warehouse, and when the lorries arrive, I stand behind them calling, "Monback!"'

An Irish inventor has come up with shovels with padded handgrips. It's not to stop Irish builders from getting blisters on their hands—it's to make the shovel more comfortable to lean on!

Did you hear about the Irishman who was so safety-conscious that he always wore white to make sure he was seen?

Unfortunately he went out one night when it was snowing and got knocked over by a snowplough!

'Paddy, did you forget to close the lion cage door last night?' shouted the circus owner when he found that 'King' the lion had gone.

'That I did, Sir,' said Paddy. 'But I thought it wouldn't matter too much. I mean who would want to steal a lion?'

Did you hear about the Irish mother who sent her son (who was in boarding school) three socks at a time instead of two?

She did it because in his last letter home, he had said that he'd grown another foot!

'Well I've stopped my Irish setter digging up the garden,' Liam told Shaun.
'How?' asked Shaun.
'I hid the shovel.'

'I hear Ol'Finbar had a heart attack and died outside a pub last night,' Pat told Paddy.
'Was he coming out or going in?' asked Paddy.
'Going in,' replied Pat.
'Oh what a shame,' said Paddy.

An Irishman was appalled when he saw his son jumping up and down on a hedgehog.

'Son!' he called. 'What on earth are you doing there?'

'Trying to get the conker out!' his son shouted back.

'Do you know I think I've got an elephant hiding underneath my bed,' Shaun told Don when they met.

'What makes you think that?' asked Don.

'Well,' said Shaun, 'when I get into bed, my nose touches the ceiling.'

An Irishman's phone was ringing, so he picked up.

'Hello, who's speaking, please?'
There was another Irish voice on the other end of the line.

'You are.'

An Irish lass asked her Gym instructor if he could teach her to do the splits.

'I can,' said the instructor, 'but I need to know how flexible you are?'
The Irish lass thought for a moment.

'I can do Mondays and Wednesdays, but I'm busy on Tuesdays.'

An Irishman was doing a crossword but was stuck on one clue, so he rang up another Irishman to see if he could help.

'What's the clue?' asked the second Irishman.

'To egg on,' replied the first Irishman.
The second Irishman thought for a while.

'Try, "Toast".'

An Irish policeman pulled O'Riley's car over and told him him that he had been driving at 50mph in a 30mph speed limit.

'I was only going 30!' O'Riley protested.

'Not according to my speedgun,' the policeman replied.

'I was only going at 30!' O'Riley shouted. The Irish policeman was starting to get annoyed. 'Look Sir, you were doing 20 miles per hour over the speed limit.'

'It's no good officer,' said Mrs O'Riley from the passenger seat. 'He won't listen. He's always like this when he's been drinking.'

There's a knock on an Irishman's door and he opens it to see a very distressed looking driver.

'I'm very sorry,' says the driver, 'but I think I've just run over your cat. I'm very sorry and I'll be more than happy to replace it.'

'Fine,' said the Irishman. 'What are you like at catching mice?'

A teacher was giving an English lesson to her class and was working on opposites.

'So what's the opposite of "Joy"?'

Claudia, a little English girl, puts up her hand.

'Is it "Sadness", Miss?'

'Well done Claudia!' says the teacher. 'Now who can tell me the opposite of "Anger"?'

Megan, a little Welsh girl, puts up her hand.

'Is it "Happiness", Miss?'

'Well done Megan!' says the teacher. 'Now who can tell me the opposite of "Woe"?'

Colleen, a little Irish girl, puts her hand up.

'Is it "Giddy Up", Miss?'

An Irishman goes to the doctor with a carrot in his ear and two chips up his nose.

'Doctor,' he says. 'I'm not feeling too good.'

'I'm not surprised,' said the doctor, 'you're not eating properly.'

An Irishman meets a leprechaun who tells him that he can have one wish.

'But remember,' says the leprechaun. 'Whatever you wish for an American will get double.'

'OK!' says the Irishman. 'Give me a million pounds and then beat me half to death.'

Three Irishmen were talking in the pub one night about the amount of control they have over their wives.

'I'll tell you what,' said one, 'just last night my wife came to me on her hands and knees.'

'Really!' said the second.

'What happened then?' asked the equally amazed third Irishman.

'She looked at me and said, "Get out from under the bed and fight like a man!"'

'So tell me about your new diet?' Nolleen asked Colleen as they sipped wine in the new film-themed wine bar Planet of the Grapes.

'Well, all I'm allowed to eat are coconuts and bananas.'

'Is that all?' asked Nolleen. 'And have you lost any weight?'

'No really,' replied Colleen, 'but you should see the way I can climb trees these days.'

An Irish girl really liked her new fridge with all its gadgets such as the computer-controlled temperature, the automatic defrosting cycle and the self-cleaning shelves. The only thing she didn't like about it was that she still had to cut the ice up into little cubes so they would fit in the trays.

An Irishman was driving from Galway to Dublin and his wife moaned at him all the way. She moaned at him when they set off, she moaned at him when they stopped half way, she moaned at him when they got to Dublin. She even moaned when he untied her from the roof rack.

An Irishman took his PC to be repaired and went to collect it.

'Have you been sending e-mails?' asked the engineer.

'Yes I have,' said the Irishman. 'How did you know?'

'I found an envelope in the CD Drive.'

Did you hear the one about the Irishman who went to PC World?

He was really disappointed when he found out that it wasn't a police theme park!

An Irish lad had met a lovely Irish lass in a nightclub and walked her home. They stood outside the door to her house.

'Thanks for a wonderful evening. Do you know you are the most wonderful girl I have ever met. You are beautiful, intelligent and funny, you don't drink, don't smoke, don't do drugs and you've just won the lotto.'

The lass smiled. 'Thank you. I'm also a very passionate woman, would you like to come in?'

The Irish lad couldn't believe his luck as the girl open the door. As he walked in to the hallway he saw a dead horse lying on the stairs.

'What's that?' he screamed.

'I never said I was tidy, did I?'

Why are tourists in Ireland like clouds?

Eventually they'll go away and you'll have a really lovely day!

An Irishwoman went to her local hospital with two very badly burned feet.

'How did that happen?' asked the nurse.

'I was making Tinned Treacle Pudding,' said the Irishwoman.

'But how did you burn your feet doing that?'

'I was only doing what it said on the tin,' replied the Irishwoman. 'It said "after opening the tin, stand in boiling water for twenty minutes".'

An Irishman books into a hotel and the porter offers to take his bags to his room. As the door closes, the Irishman looks around and starts complaining.

'Oh no, this room won't do. This isn't a double room. Where's the en-suite bathroom and the French windows and the balcony? No, this room is rubbish, I want to change it immediately.'

'This isn't your room, Sir,' said the porter. 'It's the lift.'

'I think the secret to our long marriage is because we take time to go out twice a week,' an Irishman told the newlyweds at their reception. 'It's generally a restaurant. You know, a candle-lit dinner, some good wine, some soft music and some romantic dancing.'

'That's lovely,' said the bride. 'And you do that twice a week?'

'Yes,' said the Irishman. 'She goes out on Mondays, I go out on Fridays.'

It was an Irishman's first day as a news reporter and the editor of the paper asked him a question.

'So, did you go and check out that story about the woman who could sing soprano and alto at the same time?'

'I did, Sir,' said the Irishman, 'but there was no story there. The woman just had two heads.'

An Irishman went for a job on a building site.

'So, what can you do?' asked the foreman.

'I can do brick laying, plumbing, electrics, plastering, wood work, metal work, roofing, landscaping, scaffolding, in fact anything really.'

'Oh quite a little "Bob the Builder" aren't we?' said the foreman sarcastically. 'Reckon you can do anything?'

'Yes Sir!' said the Irishman.

'Can you fetch a wheelbarrow full of wind?' the foreman asked patronisingly.

'Yes,' smiled the Irishman, 'if you fill it first.'

An Irishwoman goes into a big department store in Dublin and approaches the assistant at the haberdashery counter.

'I'd like some fur gloves, please.'

'Certainly madam,' says the assistant. 'What fur?

'To keep my hands warm of course.'

Farmer O'Dell questioned one of his Irish farmhands.

'Have you ploughed that field yet?'

'I sort of have and I've sort of not?' said the farmhand.

Farmer O'Dell was confused.

'What do you mean?'

'Well I've been thinking about it.'

'So have you ploughed the field or not?' fumed the farmer.

'No,' said the farmhand, 'but I've turned it over in my mind.'

An Irishman came home very excited.

'I've got a job!' he smiled.

'Oh well done!' said his wife. 'What is it?'

'It's a leading position within the circus.'

'A leading position. That's wonderful darling,' beamed the Irishman's wife. 'So what does that entail?'

'The elephants follow me into the ring at every show.'

After an extraordinary raid on a famous Dublin jewellers, the police questioned an Irishman who had witnessed the smash and grab.

'So just let me get this right,' said the policeman. 'You saw an elephant get out of a large van, run up to the jewellers' window and kick it in with his foot? You then saw him scoop up all the jewellery with his trunk, get back in the van and drive off?'

'That's right, Sir,' said the Irishman.

'Now tell me,' asked the policeman. 'Was it an Indian or an African elephant?'

'I don't know,' answered the Irishman. 'He had a stocking over his head.'

A man went into his local DIY shop and bought some wallpaper. At the checkout he asked the cashier, a young Irish lass:

'Can I stick the wallpaper on myself?'

'You can,' said the cashier, 'but it would look much better on the wall.'

An Irish mother was telling her teenage daughter her five secrets to a perfect relationship.

'One: find a man who helps around the house, who cooks and cleans and has a good job;

Two: find a man who can make you laugh;

Three: find a man who you can trust and you know will not lie to you;

Four: find a man who knows how to give you a good time;

'And finally,' says the Irish mother. 'Five: never let these four men meet each other.'

Did you hear about the World Tug of War Championships held in Japan?

The Irish team were disqualified for pushing!

An Irishman goes to the doctor.

'Doc I keep singing *Delilah*, *What's New Pussycat* and *The Green, Green, Grass of Home*.'

'Don't worry' said the doctor, 'you've got Tom Jones Syndrome.'

'Is that a common thing?' asks the Irishman.

'*It's Not Unusual*,' replied the doctor.

An one-eyed Irishman went into a Cork cinema.

'As I've only got one eye, do you think I could get in half price?'

'Certainly not!' said the colleen in the box office. 'In fact I should charge you double.'

'Why?' asked the Irishman.

'Because with only one eye, it'll take you twice as long to watch the whole film.'

An Irishman went into a supermarket, and was paying at the checkout. The pretty Irish girl looked at his shopping, which was made up of a tube of toothpaste, a can of beer, a meal for one, and a bag of crisps.

'You're single aren't you?' smiled the Irish girl.

'You can tell that by my shopping I suppose,' said the Irishman.

'No,' said the Irish girl, 'it's because you're so ugly.'

Once upon a time an Irish brain cell ended up in an Englishman's head. The brain cell looked around, but couldn't see any other brain cells. In fact the head was empty. The Irish brain cell was getting a little scared so it called out.

'Hello, is anybody there?' Then it heard a voice from far, far below it.

'Hello, we're down here...'

A little Irish girl came into the living room.

'Mammy we can go to bed now, Daddy's locked up for the night.'
The little Irish girl's mammy smiled. 'I don't think so poppet, Daddy isn't home yet.'

'I know,' said the little Irish girl, 'but the police have just rung to say that Daddy's locked up for the night.'

An Irishwoman watched as her husband's coffin was lowered into the ground and sobbed on a relative's shoulder.

'Oh I really blame myself for his death.'

'Oh come on,' comforted the relative. 'Why on earth would you think that?'

'Because I shot him!' wept the Irishwoman.

Did you hear about the Irishman who went to a mind reader?

She gave him his money back after 30 seconds!

An old Irishman was lying on his deathbed when he could smell his wife's cooking. He opened his eyes and called for his wife, who rushed to his side.

'What are you cooking?' he asked.

'A cake,' said his wife.

'Well, you know I'm not long for this world now, but before I go could I have one last taste of your cooking?'

'What would you like?' asked his wife.

'What about some of that cake? It smells wonderful.'

'Oh you can't have that,' said his wife. 'That's for the funeral.'

An Irishman is walking down the street and about ten feet away he sees a banana skin on the pavement.

'Oh no,' he groans. 'Here we go again.'

A tourist was fishing in an Irish river when an Irishman came up and started watching him. He didn't speak to or bother the tourist or say a word at all. He just watched. Three hours passed.

'You've been standing there all afternoon watching me. Why don't you have a go at fishing yourself?'

'No thanks,' said the Irishman. 'I haven't got the patience.'

Farmer O'Dell spoke to one of his farmhands,

'Did you count the pigs this morning?'

'I did Sir,' said the farmhand. 'I counted 24.'

'24?' Farmer O'Dell said. 'There's supposed to be 25.'

'Ah now, that must have been the little blighter I saw run off before I'd finished counting.'

An Irishman was taking part in a pub quiz and it was his question.

'OK,' said the Question master. 'This is a question in three parts. Part one; who succeeded Henry the eighth?'

'Edward the sixth,' said the Irishman.

'Correct. Part two of the question: Who reigned after Edward the sixth?'

'Mary,' replied the Irishman.

'Correct again,' said the Question master. 'Here is the final part: Who followed Mary?'

'Her little lamb!'

'Bonjour!' said the Frenchman to the Irishman, who asked, 'What does that mean?'

'In France it means "Good Day".'

'Oh right,' said the Irishman. 'Well, Hot Cross Buns.'

'What does that mean?' asked the Frenchman.

'In Ireland it means "Good Friday".'

Two old Irishmen, Clancy and Delaney shared an ancient two-roomed farmhouse somewhere way down west. When Clancy went to see relatives they asked him how things were going.

'Oh Delaney is very difficult to live with. He keeps sheep in the kitchen, goats in the bedroom and pigs in the bathroom. The smell is awful.'

'Why don't you open a window?' said the relative.

'What and let all my pigeons escape?' snapped Clancy.

Farmer O'Dingle is leaning on his gate when a man walks up to him.

'Excuse me,' says the man. 'Could you tell me the quickest way to Dublin?'

'Are you walking or driving?' asks the farmer.

'Driving,' answered the man.

'Well I'd say that that was the quickest way.'

An Irishman and a monkey were to be the only life forms on the first ever Space Shuttle to Mars. On entering the shuttle they found two envelopes marked 'Monkey' and 'Irishman.'

The monkey opened his envelope—a letter containing complicated and precise details of not only how to pilot the shuttle, but all the aims and expectations of the voyage.

The Irishman opened his envelope. The piece of paper read: 'Feed the monkey.'

An Irish drunk stumbles onto the bus and sits in a seat next to a priest. Smelling his breath and seeing the state he's in, the priest says,

'Sir, do you not realise that you are on the road to perdition?'

'I am?' burps the Irishman. 'I could have sworn this was the bus for Wexford.'

An Irishman's dad was very ill. The doctors had done all they could for him—the priest told him that the only thing that could save him was a miracle and suggested a trip to Lourdes.

So the Irishman and all his friends had a whip round and off the Irishman and his dad went. A week later the priest met him and asked how the trip went.

'He died about an hour after we arrived,' said the Irishman.

'Oh I'm sorry,' comforted the priest. 'Perhaps it was God's way of stopping his suffering.'

'I don't think so, Father,' said the Irishman. 'I think it was more to do with the speed the cricket ball was travelling when it hit him on the head.'

An Irishman pops into his local greengrocers.

'Four pound of potatoes, please.'

The greengrocer shakes his head. 'Sorry I can't do that. It's all kilos now, I'm afraid.'

'Oh I see?' says the Irishman. 'I'll have four pound of kilos, then.'

An Irishman had been going to evening classes to better himself. His wife rang the college up to see how he was doing.

'He's doing quite well; he's been making straight As,' the tutor said.
The Irishman's wife was absolutely delighted.

'That's wonderful!' she said.

'It is,' replied the teacher. 'Next week, we're going to work on his wonky Bs.'

An Englishman, a bit the worse for drink, stood up in the middle of a Dublin pub and shouted at the top of his voice.

'I was born an Englishman, I shall live my life as an Englishman and by God I shall die an Englishman.'

An Irishman shouted from the back of the bar.

'For pity's sake, man! Have you no ambition?'

An Irish lad went up to a lovely Irish lass at a party.

'Do you know I think you're the most beautiful girl here tonight?'

'Thank you,' said the girl uninterestedly.

'Could I call you later?' asked the Irish lad.

'I suppose so,' mumbled the Irish lass.

'Great! What's your number?' he asked eagerly.

'It's in the phone book.'

'Right!' smiled the Irish lad. 'So, what's your name?'

'That's in the phone book as well,' said the Irish lass before she walked away.

Milly O'Silly was a maid in a big house when the mistress called her into the lounge.

'Milly!' said the mistress as she stood by the grand piano. 'Look at this piano, it's so dirty. Why, I could write my name in the dust.'

'Oh Mam,' smiled Milly, 'that's education for you.'

An Irishman visited his doctor complaining of pains in his knees. The doctor examined him.

'You're suffering from a condition called 'Kneesitis'. I suggest you take it easy for a month, rest your knees and above all don't climb any stairs, as this will put strain on your knee joints.'

After a month the Irishman went back to the doctor and after a brief examination was told that his knees were back to normal.

'Oh that's great!' said the Irishman. 'Does that mean I can climb stairs again?'

'It certainly does,' replied the doctor.

'Thank God for that. I was getting fed up having to climb the drainpipe every time I wanted to go to the toilet.'

Did you hear about the Irishman who bought his wife a rocket for her birthday?

She was over the moon!

An Irishman comes home late from work one night and his wife is there to greet him.

'Hi dear,' she says. 'Notice anything different about me tonight?'

'You've had your hair done.'

'No,' says his wife. 'Try again.'

'You're wearing a new dress?'

'No,' said the wife slightly disappointed. 'Try again.'

'Oh I'm too tired to play this stupid game!' snapped the Irishman. 'I give up.'

'I'm wearing a gas mask!'

Irish plumber Fixus McLeek and his mate knocked on the front door of the big house.

'Did you phone for a plumber, missus?'

'I did,' said the lady. 'But that was in January, nearly six months ago.'

'Oh sorry missus!' he apologised, then turned to his mate. 'It's the wrong house Pat; the woman we're looking for phoned in December.'

Paddy, Mick and Shamus take an intelligence test prior to working on the building site.

'OK Paddy,' says the foreman. 'What is three times three?'

'Now, Sir, that would be four thousand and sixty two.'

'Not quite,' says the foreman. It's Mick's turn. 'What's three times three?'

Mick thinks, then says 'Friday.'

'Not even close!' replies the foreman and then finally asks Shamus. 'What's three times three?'

Shamus thinks long and hard and then says, 'Nine.'

'Correct!' exclaims the foreman. 'And how did you work that out?'

'Easy,' said Shamus. 'I just subtracted four thousand and sixty-two from Friday.'

A tourist walking through the Irish countryside stopped to ask the Irish farmer what he was building.

'Well Sir, if I can rent it out,' said the Irish farmer, 'it's a rustic Irish holiday cottage. And if I can't, it's a cow shed.'

An Irishman was doing his first parachute jump. At 30,000 feet his parachute wouldn't open. As he plummeted downwards, he saw another Irishman soaring upwards.

'Here,' he called, 'do you know anything about parachutes?'

'No,' said the other Irishman. 'Do you know anything about gas cookers?'

An Irishman went into a pet shop to buy some birdseed. The shopkeeper handed over a packet.

'So how deep do I plant them, and how long will it be before I grow some birds?'

A man went into a Belfast fish and chip shop.

'Fish and chips twice, please.'

The woman behind the counter looked up from the frier.

'It's OK, I heard you the first time.'

An Irishman is concerned because his wife thinks she is a washing line.

'Very strange,' says the doctor. 'You'd best bring her in.'

'What and have all my washing fall on the ground?'

Did you hear about the Irish builder who didn't know the difference between toothpaste and putty?

He slammed the door at home once and all his windows fell out!

Did you hear about the Irishman who decided to go on a hitch-hiking holiday?

He left early to avoid the traffic!

An Irishman was leaving a restaurant.

'Excuse me, waiter. Have you seen my hat?'

'It's on your head, Sir.'

'Don't bother then,' said the Irishman. 'I'll look for it myself.'

An Irishwoman went into her local baker's and asked for a loaf of bread.

'I'm afraid that bread has gone up another 10p today,' said the baker.

'Oh dear, has it?' said the Irishwoman. 'Well in that case give me one of yesterday's loaves.'

'Why don't you go out and find some work?' a fed up Irishwoman said to her idle husband.

'I can't; I'm frightened!' said her husband.

'Frightened of what?' asked the Irishwoman.

'Finding some.'

Did you hear about the Irishman who was really tight with money?

He sent his brother, who lived in Liverpool, a homing pigeon for his birthday!

A man was being trained by the Irish Parachute Team and was about to jump.

'What happens if my parachute doesn't open?'

'Bring it back and we'll replace it!' shouted the instructor.

'So Pat, how long did you work last week?'

'One day,' replied Pat.
His friend sighed.

'Oh it must be nice to have a steady job like that.'

Detective O'Malley arrived at the scene of the crime and approached the Irish policeman on duty.

'Was the victim seriously wounded?'

'Well, Sir, two of the injuries were fatal, but the third was just a flesh wound.'

An Irishwoman went shopping at the new supermarket.

'I'd like some pepper, please.'

'Certainly, Miss,' said the assistant. 'What sort; Ground, Seeds, Black or Cayenne?'

'Toilet.'

Whilst on holiday in Ireland, an Englishman has a slow puncture in one of his tyres, so he pulls in to a service station.

'I say my good man, what do you have in the shape of tyres?'
The Irishman behind the counter thinks for a moment.

'Doughnuts, pancakes, biscuits, CDs and a couple of kid's hoops in the toy section.'

Two Irishmen were sitting on a train.

'Does this train stop at Waterford?'
'It does,' said the other.
'When?' asked the first Irishman.
'Oh, just watch me,' said the other Irishman, 'and get off two stops before I do.'

'Doc, you've got to help me!' said an Irishman. 'I snore so loud at night that I keep waking myself up. What do you suggest?'

'Have you tried sleeping in another room?'

'I have,' the Irishman sighed. 'But I can still hear myself.'

Two Irish fashion designers were on holiday in Africa, and were walking past a river when they saw a crocodile swim past with a man's head in its mouth.

'Oh bejabers!' said one of the designers. 'Did you see that?'

'I did!' replied the second designer. 'I never knew that Lacoste did sleeping bags.'

No one was saying that Phil O'Food wasn't suited for his job in the restaurant kitchen, but on his first day the chef caught him trying to open an egg with a tin opener.

An English foreman was employing labourers, but didn't want any Irishmen. So when Paddy arrived he decided to give him a test that he wouldn't be able to complete.

'OK Paddy,' he said. 'Without using numbers, I want you to represent the number 9 on this piece of paper.'

'OK Sir,' said Paddy and proceeded to draw a trio of trees.

'What's that?' the foreman asked.

'Three trees,' said Paddy, 'and three trees make nine.'

'Oh right!' replied the foreman. 'I now want you to do the same again, but this time I want you to represent 99.'

Convinced that he had got the Irishman this time, he watched as Paddy smudged his drawing.

'What's that?' he asked again.

'Well Sir, I've made the trees dirty. As anyone can tell you, dirty tree and dirty tree and dirty tree makes 99.'

So the foreman gave the Irishman the job!

'Excuse me, do you serve women in this pub?' the Irishman asked the landlord.
'No we don't, Sir,' said the landlord. 'You have to bring your own.'

An Irishman went in to a hotel and saw a sign that said "Please ring the bell for the receptionist". He rang it, and the receptionist duly arrived.
'Now, why can't you ring that little bell yourself?' the Irishman asked.

Carrie Cash went into her local cheese shop.
'I'd like your strongest Irish cheese, please.'
The shopkeeper called out to the back of the shop.
'Are you there Margaret? Unchain number 26.'

one about the unlucky
d the navy to see the

on a submarine!

see the doctor about his

counting sheep?' the

boxer, 'but whenever I

ing his dog through the
w another man.
man.
, 'just walking the dog.'

Did you hear the one about the Irishman who was absolutely useless at cards?

Every time he was dealt a spade, he'd spit on his hands and rub them together!

'Have you seen my boots?' the Irishman asked his wife.

'No I haven't,' answered his wife. 'Are you sure you had them on when you took them off?'

An Irish girl went in to Boots and asked for a bar of soap.

'Would you like it scented?' asked the lady on the counter.

'No thanks,' said the girl. 'I'll take it with me.'

An American went to Dublin market. At a fruit and veg stall he picked up a melon.

'Hey Buddy,' he said sarcastically to the Irish stallholder, 'are these the biggest apples you do?'

'Here you, put that grape down!'

Did you hear the one about the Irishman who broke the world 100 metre record whilst wearing his walking boots?

He fell off a cliff!

An Irishman was taking his first ever trip on a train when the ticket collector approached him.

'Ticket please.'

'No way!' said the Irishman. 'I've paid for mine, you get your own.'

An Irishman was having his flying lesson when the instructor turned to him.

'You're doing so well, tomorrow you will fly solo.'

'How low is that then?' asked the Irishman.

Did you hear the one about the Irish motor mechanic who started drinking brake fluid?

He drank so much of the stuff that his boss was worried that he was becoming addicted to it.

'I'm not addicted to it,' he told his boss. 'I can stop anytime!'

A man was staying in a hotel in Dublin when he received a call from the reception desk.

'Excuse me, Sir,' said the soft Irish voice on the other end of the phone. 'This is Jilly on reception. Sorry to bother you, but what time did you want calling this morning? Was it seven o'clock or eight o'clock?'

'Er, what's the time now?' asked the man.

'Twenty to ten.'

Why aren't Irishmen allowed to hold car-boot sales?

They keep selling the engines of the cars that have been reversed in!

Two priests are standing on the road holding up two signs that read:

'The End Is Near.' and
'Turn back before it's too late.'

A car approaches and the driver winds down his window and shouts.

'Get off the road and get back in church, yer eejits.'

The car screeches on past them and around the bend in the road. Suddenly there is a screech of tyres and a big splash. One priest says to the other

'Do you think we should change the signs to just say BRIDGE OUT?'

A drunk Irishman was walking down a Dublin street shouting at everyone he passed.

'Sage! Parsley! Thyme! Rosemary! Sage! Parsley! Thyme! Rosemary!'

He was later arrested for 'Herbal Abuse'.

'What happened to you?' the Irishman's wife asked him when he arrived home soaking wet. 'Is it raining?'

'No it isn't,' he said, 'but that's the last time I take my motorbike through that car wash.'

An Irishman went horse riding the other week, but never again. It all started off fine. The Irishman got on the horse, held onto the reins, but then the horse started bouncing out of control. The Irishman tried to hang on, but the horse was bucking so much that he fell off. Unfortunately for the Irishman, his foot got caught in a stirrup and he hit his head on the ground as the horse refused to stop or slow down. Slowly, and with colossal effort, the Irishman managed to pull himself up by grabbing hold of the stirrup. He was almost back in the saddle when suddenly... the shop manager came and turned the ride off!

'So how're you getting on selling your old car?' Thaddy asked.

'Not very well,' said Paddy, 'on account of it having 195,000 miles on the clock.'

'Don't worry about that,' said Thaddy. 'I've got a mate who works in a garage who will turn the clock back to 50,000 miles for a couple of pounds.'

The following week Thaddy and Paddy met again.

'Did you take your car to my mate?'

'Yeah!' smiled Paddy.

'Did he put the mileage back?'

'He certainly did.' Paddy smiled even more.

'And have you sold the car now?' Thaddy enquired.

'No,' replied Paddy.

'Why not?' asked Thaddy.

'Didn't see the point. It only had 50,000 on the clock.'

'Doctor. I'm really worried about my brother,' the Irish girl said. 'He thinks he's an apple.'

'Oh dear,' said the doctor. 'I think I'd best have a look at him. Is he with you today?'

'Yes,' said the Irish girl.

'Is he in the waiting room?' asked the doctor.

'No,' said the Irish girl. 'He's in my pocket.'

An Irish boy bought his girlfriend her first mobile phone for her birthday. The next day she was out shopping and her phone rang. It was the Irish boy.

'Hi dear. How do you like your new phone?'

'It's wonderful,' said the Irish girl. 'But there's just one thing I don't understand?'

'What's that sweetheart?' asked the Irish boy.

'How did you know I would be here?'

Another Drop of Irish Jokes

An Irishman had got a ticket to the Ireland rugby match, but when he got to the packed ground he found he was right at the back of the stand. He looked around and there, right at the front of the terrace was another Irishman sitting next to an empty chair.

The Irishman jostled his way to the front and asked the man if he could sit in the empty chair.

'Sure,' said his fellow Irishman. 'It was my wife's seat. We always used to watch this fixture, year after year, but she passed away, shortly after I bought the tickets.'

'Oh I'm sorry,' said the Irishman, 'but couldn't you have given the ticket to a friend or a relative, so you wouldn't be alone?'

'Not today,' sighed the other Irishman. 'They're all at her funeral.'

135

Pat comes rushing home from school one day.

'Mammy, we learnt to count at school today. All the other boys only counted to 5, but I counted to 10.'

'Well done!' said Pat's mammy.

'Is that because I'm Irish, Mammy?' he beamed.

'Yes darling, it is because you're Irish.'

'Another thing we did today was the alphabet. All the other boys only got to D, but I got to L.'

'Excellent!' said Pat's mammy.

'Is that because I'm Irish, Mammy?' he beamed.

'Yes darling, it is because you're Irish.'

'Oh and when we went swimming, mammy, I had a hairy chest, but the other boys didn't. Is that because I'm Irish, Mammy?'

'No darling,' said Pat's mammy. 'It's because you're 26.'

'Is your car OK now?' asked Mary as she and Colleen met up in local Charles Dickens themed wine bar 'Grape Expectations'.

'Yes, thank goodness!' said Colleen. 'To be honest I thought the mechanic would try and rip me off because I was a blonde Irishwoman.'

'And did he?'

'No he didn't!' beamed Colleen. 'I was so relieved when he only charged me £40 for new indicator fluid.'

Did you hear about the Irishman who complained to the Irish TV network about all the sex, nudity, foul language and violence on television?

It was actually the tape on his video recorder!

An Irishman was in hospital awaiting a brain operation, but wanted a word with the surgeon.

'What seems to be the problem?'

'Well, I've just been speaking to the English guy in the next bed,' said the Irishman. 'He's having the same operation as me, and it's costing him £1000 less than mine. So what I want to know is why you charge me more?'

'You're Irish,' said the Surgeon.

'What's that got to do with it?' asked the Irishman.

'We always charge a search fee.'

An Irishman goes into a bar and orders 9 pints of stout. To the amazement of the barman he drinks them down one after the other.

'Ah that was great,' says the Irishman wiping his mouth. 'But I shouldn't have done that with what I've got.'

'Why, what have you got?' asked the barman.

'About a pound.'

An elderly Irish couple are on holiday in Wales when they come across and road sign that read

"Llanfairpwllgwyngyllgogerychwyrndrobwllllan tysiliogogogoch"

Both try to pronounce it, but end up arguing. They are still arguing when they go into a restaurant in the town for lunch. The waiter appears to take their order.

'We're from Ireland and we were just wondering how you pronounce where we are?'

'And could you do it slowly?' adds the wife.

The waiter shrugs his shoulders.

'Liiiiiiitttttttllllleeee Chhhheeeeeffffffffff!'

The manager of the Kilkenny Social Club is woken up by a 3am phone call.

'What time does the club open?' the voice slurred.

'Midday!' said the manager and hung up. An hour later the phone rang again—it was the same person.

'What time does the club open?'

'Like I said earlier!' snapped the manager. 'Midday.' Again she slammed the phone down. At 5:30am the phone rang again and the mumbling voice sounded even more drunk.

'Excuse me Miss, but what time did you say that the club opened?'

'Look I've already told you twice: Midday.' The manager shouted angrily down the line. 'And if you don't sober up, you won't be allowed in.'

'In?' said the voice. 'I don't want to get in, I want to get out.'

The Irishman asked his dying mother if she would like to be buried or cremated.

'Oh I don't know, son,' said his mother. 'Surprise me!'

An Irishman was the first human ever to undergo a tortoise heart transplant. The operation was a complete success, and he was able to leave hospital a month later.

Three weeks after that, he reached the car park!

Did you hear the one about the dyslexic Irish twins?

Every full moon one changed into a warehouse, and his brother became an atheist who didn't believe in dog!

Paddy and Pat had gone out hunting, but got lost as it started to get dark. Paddy mentioned that he read somewhere that the best thing to do was to stay in one place, fire three shots and wait for someone to find you.

So that's what they did.

Two hours passed and still nobody had come. So Paddy suggested that they fire another three shots into the night sky and wait.

Three hours passed and still nothing.

'Fire three more shots,' said Paddy.

'OK,' said Pat, 'but I hope someone comes soon—we're running out of arrows.'

There was a knock on an Irishman's door one morning. When he opened it, a very angry neighbour confronted him.

'I left my house to go for a newspaper and that dog of yours went for me!' he snapped.

'Well would you believe it?' said the Irishman. 'I've had that dog for ten years. I've fed it, looked after it, walked it and in all that time it's never once got the paper for me.'

Liam and Shaun were sitting in a pub. The wall opposite them had a very large mirror on it.

'Here Shaun,' said Liam. 'Don't look now, but there are a couple of fellas over there the spitting image of you and me.'
Shaun looked over and was astonished.

'So they are. Same clothes, same hair. That's amazing!'

'I tell you what,' said Liam standing up. 'I'm going to buy them a drink.'

'No sit down, Liam,' whispered Shaun. 'The one that looks like you is coming over.'

Paddy's mammy rang him at home one evening.

'Paddy, your sister has had a baby!' she said excitedly.

'Oh that's great, Mammy,' replied Paddy.

'I haven't found out yet, if it's a boy or a girl,' his mammy told him, 'so I can't tell you if you're an uncle or aunt.'

A TV documentary had shown a couple of anglers in Scotland catching salmon, one holding the legs of the other while he dangled over a bridge, catching fish as they swam up river. Thinking this an excellent idea, Liam and Shaun decided to try it themselves.

They found a bridge. Liam dangled Shaun over. About half an hour passed.

'Liam, Liam, pull me up quick!'

'Have you caught a salmon, Shaun?' Liam asked excitedly.

'Not yet. There's a train coming.'

Paddy O'Pudding, Ireland's fattest man, fell into the crocodile enclosure at Dublin Zoo. The keepers did all they could, but by the time they hoisted him out, he had eaten three crocodiles.

'I'm not going to my local hospital anymore!' the Irishman said.

'Why not?' asked his wife.

'Well I went there today and there was a sign on the door: "Guide Dogs operating here." I know they're clever and everything, but there's got to be a limit.'

'Mammy, I think you might be colour blind,' said the little Irish girl as she started to eat her dessert.

'I don't think so,' said her Mammy. 'What makes you say that?'

'This rhubarb tart has got celery in it.'

The Irish mathematics teacher stood up in front of the class.

'There are three types of people in this world: those who can count and those who can't.'

An Irishman went for a job as a tree feller and on his first day chopped down an amazing 200 trees. The foreman was very, very impressed.

'Hey, that's fantastic work. Where did you learn to cut down trees like that?'

'In the Sahara Forest,' replied the Irishman.

'Surely you mean the Sahara Desert?' said the Foreman.

'Well, that's what they call it now.'

Barry and Carrie were getting married. The guests were going into the church and the ushers were showing them to their seats.

'Would you be a friend of the groom?' asked the chief usher.

'Certainly not!' snapped the lady. 'I'm the mother of the bride.'

An Irish girl was crying at her work desk. Her boss asked what was wrong.

'I got a phone call this morning from my Da saying that my Mammy has died.'

'Oh I'm so sorry. Look why don't you take the day off?'

'No thank you,' sniffed the Irish girl. 'Being here helps me to take my mind off things for a while.'

'Are you sure?'

'Yes, thank you, I'll be fine now I've had a good cry.'

Hoping she was OK the boss returned to his office. Ten minutes later he was told that the Irish girl is sobbing her heart out again.

'What's the matter?' he asked.

'Oh it's awful, I can't take much more,' the Irish girl sobbed.

'What is it?' The boss asked anxiously.

'My sister has just rung and… and… her Mammy has just died too,' the Irish girl wailed.

An Irish girl went for a job interview and the interviewer asked her age.

'Let me see,' she said, as she started counting on her fingers, then slipped off her shoes and counted her toes. '19.'

'OK,' said the interviewer. 'And how tall are you?'

The girl reached into her handbag, took out a tape measure and measured herself. 'I'm 5ft 3 inches tall,' she smiled.

'What's your name?'

'Oh, I know this one! Just hang on a minute, it'll come to me. Now let's see…
Happy Birthday to me, Happy Birthday to me, Happy Birthday dear…Mary!'

'I hope you don't mind me asking but what's that on the side of your face?' an Irishman asked a man he had just met.

'Not at all,' replied the man. 'It's a birthmark.'

'Oh I see!' said the Irishman. 'And how long have you had that then?'

An Irishman was sitting in front of an old Irish biddy on a long coach journey. During the ride she tapped him on the shoulder and offered him a handful of peanuts, which he accepted, as he was hungry. About 15 minutes later she did the same, tapped the Irishman on the shoulder and gave him some peanuts. She did this a number of times throughout the trip. When the coach reached its final destination and the old biddy had given the Irishman her last handful of peanuts, he was curious.

'Why did you keep giving me all those peanuts?'

'Well because with my old teeth, I can't eat them,' she grinned.

'Why did you buy them, then?' asked the Irishman.

'Because I like licking off the chocolate coating.'

Two Irishmen were playing golf. They were on the eighteenth hole and one was taking a very long time before he played the shot.

'Come on. What you playing at?' said his friend.

'I want this to be my best shot ever. My wife is watching me from the clubhouse steps.'

'Oh don't be stupid,' said his friend. 'You'll never hit her from here.'

An Irishman went to Las Vegas and tried his luck on the roulette table. He placed his first bet on number 7 and lost. He put more money on number 7, and lost again. Next time round, he chose number 7, placed his bet and lost. Finally, with only a few dollars left, he was about to place a final bet on number 7 when another gambler said:

'Why don't you try a different number?'

'Are you joking?' said the Irishman. 'Seven is my lucky number!'

Dolan was always late for work because he overslept. His boss warned him that if he didn't do something about it, he would be fired. So Dolan went to his doctor who gave him a pill to take just before he went to bed. Dolan slept really well and was up before the alarm went off. He was up so early that he had time to have breakfast and walk to work. He was even at his desk before his boss arrived.

'Morning boss!' Dolan grinned and told him all about the pill.

'That's all very well, Dolan,' said his boss. 'But where were you yesterday?'

Did you hear the one about the Irishman who called 3am in the morning 'A pig's tail'?

Well, it was twirly!

An Irishman was very worried about the truck he was driving behind and tried desperately to get the driver to stop. Finally the truck came to some traffic lights and stopped. An Irishman jumped out and in a panic rushed up to the driver's door.

'What's the matter?' asked the driver.

'I tried to stop you earlier!' the Irishman said urgently. 'It's your load; you're losing it. It's going all over the road.'

The driver gave a look.

'I drive a gritter.'

A blind Irishman and his guide dog walk into a shop. He stops, picks up his dog by its lead and starts swinging it around his head.

'Excuse me, Sir,' says a concerned shop assistant. 'Can I help you?'

'No thanks,' said the blind Irishman. 'I'm just having a look around.'

An Irishman wanted to start his own zoo so he wrote to his local pet store. He wasn't sure if he was using the correct collective noun when he asked for two mongooses. He tried two 'mongi', but that didn't sound right; and he tried 'mongeeses' and that didn't sound any better. In the end he wrote this letter:

'Dear Sir,

I am starting my own zoo. Please can you send me a mongoose?

PS: And can you send me another one as well?'

The young Irishwoman was distraught when the policeman turned up after she had called to say that her car had been broken into.

'I don't believe it!' she wailed. 'They've taken the CD player, the radio, the steering wheel, the glove compartment, the dash board, the gear stick...'

'Madam, let's calm down. Would you like to get out of the back seat?'

It was 2am when Bob's wife woke him up, telling him that someone was knocking on the front door. Bob got up, trudged downstairs and opened the door. Standing on the doorstep was a drunk Irishman.

'Sorry to disturb you Sir, so I am, but do you think you could give me a push?'

'Do you know what time it is?' snapped Bob. 'Go away.' He slammed the door and went back to bed.

'Oh that wasn't very nice,' said his wife when he told her. 'Remember that time we were on holiday in Ireland and our car broke down? That kind Irishman gave us a push.'

'OK, OK,' said Bob as he went back downstairs and opened the door. He couldn't see anyone, but called out.

'Do you still want a push?'

'Yes please,' slurred an Irish voice.

'Where are you?' Bob called again.

'Over here!' called the drunken Irishman. 'On the swing.'

Farmer O'Dell and Farmer O'Dingle were driving their tractor down the middle of a narrow country road. Suddenly a car comes around the corner: the driver sees the tractor and slams on the brakes to avoid it. The car skids, hits an embankment, flips over a couple of times and lands in a field where the driver crawls out through the window .

'That's lucky,' said Farmer O'Dell. 'A couple of minutes earlier and we would still be in that field.'

Why are Irish jokes so simple?

So that everybody else in the world can understand them!

'Well I know that!' shouted the Irish office worker. 'What do you think I am? An eejit?' She slammed down the phone just as her boss walked past.

'Is there a problem?' he asked.

'Not really,' she replied. 'Just some bozo telling me it's a long distance from Australia.'

'How much are your chickens?' a customer asked Farmer O'Dell.

'They're £7,' said the Farmer.

'And did you raise them yourself?'

'Oh yes,' said Farmer O'Dell. 'Yesterday they were £6.'

Liam was telling Shaun how he played Scrabble with his pet dog.

'Wow!' said Shaun. 'That's one clever dog.'

'Not really,' replied Liam. 'I've beaten him a couple of times and his spelling isn't that good.'

Three long time friends, an Englishman, a Scotsman and an Irishman were stranded on Desert Island when they found a Genie in a bottle. The Genie told the men that they could have one wish each.

'I wish I was playing for England in the World cup final, just about to score the winning goal.'

The Genie clapped his hands, and there was the Englishman just about to receive a perfect cross from David Beckham. Back on the island the Scotsman was next.

'I wish I was playing for Scotland in the World Rugby cup final and I was just about to score the winning try against the Australians.'

The Genie clapped his hands, and there was the Scotsman running with the ball under his arm towards the line.

'OK, your turn!' the Genie said to the Irishman. 'What do you want?'
The Irishman thought for a while.

'Well now everyone's gone, I'm really lonely. I wish my friends were with me.'

157

An Irishman had promised his wife he would give up the drink, although he had been drinking heavily in the pub and it was now time to go home.

He stood up to go and promptly fell to the floor. Picking himself up and using chairs and tables, he wobbled to the door of the pub, opened it and fell into the street. No matter how much he tried, every time he managed to stand up, he fell flat on his face.

Eventually the Irishman crawled home, managing to open his front door before he fell into his house. He crawled up the stairs and into his bedroom where his wife was sleeping. With one last effort the Irishman stood up, wobbled then fell onto the bed and into a deep sleep.

When he woke next morning his wife was standing over him.

'You've been drinking, haven't you?'

'What makes you think that, dearest?' asked the bleary-eyed Irishman.

'Because the pub's just phoned to say that you left your crutches there again last night!'

An Irish girl was on holiday. She was lying on her front while sunbathing, when a little boy walked past. He accidentally dropped his ice cream on her back. She screamed.

'Bejabers, those seagulls must live in a freezer.'

A tourist was talking to an Irishman in a pub one day.

'Why do you Irish people talk in questions?'
The Irishman thought for a while.

'Do we? Is that so? Well, whoever would have guessed?'

'Here, I've given up betting,' said the Irishman.
'Bet you haven't.'
'Bet you, I have.'
'How much?'
'Ten pounds?'

Paddy was busy digging a hole on a Dublin building site when his foreman came up and asked if he would like to buy a raffle ticket.

'What for?' asked Paddy.

'You know the crane driver suddenly died of a heart attack last week?'

'Yes,' said Paddy.

'Well it's for his wife and five kids.'

'Oh, no thanks then,' replied Paddy. 'I've already got a wife and kids and I don't want to win anymore.'

An Irishman was talking to another about an article in the paper.

'It said that one in five people in the world are Chinese and there are five people in my family.'

'So?' said his friend.

'Well that means one of them must be Chinese. I know it's not me, so it's either me Mam and Da or me little sister Mary, or my older brother Ho-Chin-Lou. So I reckon it must be Mary.'

'Well,' said the doctor to the Irishman. 'I've given you a thorough examination and I think you should give up the stout, the women, the gambling and the singing.'

'Oh I see,' says the concerned Irishman. 'Will that help me live longer?'

'Well,' the doctor replied, 'it will certainly feel like it.'

'What happened?' an Irishman asked his neighbour when he saw him on crutches with his leg in plaster.

'I broke it playing table tennis,' said his neighbour.

'Playing table tennis?' the Irishman laughed. 'How did you manage that?'

'Well, I won and tried to jump the net.'

An Irishman went into a restaurant and ordered lobster. When it arrived, he wasn't happy and called over the waiter.

'This lobster has only got one claw!' he complained.

'I know Sir,' sniffed the waiter. 'He lost it in a fight.'

'Well take this one back,' snapped the Irishman, 'and bring me the winner.'

Old Mrs Kelly answered the door to a man who asked after her husband.

'Is Mr Kelly in?'

'I'm afraid he's dead,' said old Mrs Kelly.

'Oh I'm so sorry to hear that,' replied the man. 'When did he die?'

'Well,' began old Mrs Kelly, 'if he had lived 'til tomorrow, he'd have been dead for a fortnight.'

A woman goes into a shop and asks for an Irish sausage.

'Are you Irish?' asked the shop assistant.

'I am, but I don't see what that has to do with it. If I asked for a German sausage, would you ask me if I was German? If I asked for an Italian sausage would you assume I was Italian?'

'Well, no,' said the shop assistant.

'So why, when I ask for an Irish sausage, do you ask me if I'm Irish?'

'Because this is a book shop!'

There was a fatal accident at the Dublin Distillery last week. Pat O'Butter fell into a giant vat of Irish whiskey. His work colleagues tried to save him, but he fought them off bravely.
He drowned, eventually, after getting out three times to go to the toilet.
After his funeral he was cremated, and it took four days to put the fire out.

Two Irish mothers were talking, when the first told the second that she had ten children, all boys.

'Ten!' said the other mother. 'What's their names?'

'Patrick, Patrick, Patrick, Patrick, Patrick, Patrick, Patrick, Patrick, Patrick and Patrick.'

'Why did you give them all the same name?' asked the second mother.

'To make life simple!' said the first mother. 'If I want them to come in from playing I just shout "Patrick"; and they all come. If I want them to come to dinner I just shout "Patrick" and they all come.'

'But what if you only want one of them?' said the second woman.

'Oh that's when it gets a bit difficult; then I have to use their surname as well.'

An Irish workman walks into a pub with a rolled up strip of tarmac under his arm.

'Pint of the black stuff, please, and one for the road.'

'Daddy, I'm going to ask Father Christmas for "Divorced Barbie",' said the little Irish girl.

'Why?' asked her dad.

'Because with "Divorced Barbie" you not only get all her clothes, but you get all Ken's clothes, Ken's car, Ken's boat and Ken's House.'

'I've finally found out that me and the wife have something in common,' an Irishman told his friend.

'And what's that?'

'We were married on the same day.'

'Have you seen these new Irish Whiskey bottles?' Liam asked Shaun.

'No,' said Shaun. 'What's different about them?'

'Well they've got instructions on the bottom and top of the bottle. On the bottom of this one it says "Open other end".'

'And what does it say on the top?' asked Shaun.

'"See other end for instructions".'

An Irishman had nearly completed his driving test. The driving instructor was asking him some road sign questions.

'OK. What does an unbroken single yellow line mean?'

'No parking at all,' said the Irishman.

'Well done! Now what does two unbroken yellow lines mean?'

The Irishman thought for a while.

'No parking at all, at all.'

Three old Irish biddies, Mary, Martha and Marie, were sitting in Mary's kitchen talking about getting old.

'It's getting terrible,' says Mary. 'I go to the cupboard with a pot of jam and I can't remember if I'm putting it away or making a sandwich!'

'Me too,' adds Martha. 'I sometimes find myself half way up the stairs, wondering if I'm going up or down.'

'Well I must be lucky,' says Marie. 'I don't suffer from those sort of problems, touch wood.' She taps the table. 'Did you hear that? Someone must be at the door, I'll just go and get it.'

It was an Irish girl's first time on a plane. No sooner had she sat in a nice window seat than a man came up to her and said that she was sitting in his seat.

'I'm not!' protested the Irish girl.

'You are,' repeated the man.

'Well I don't think I am!' snapped the Irish girl. 'I'm not for moving.'

The man held up his hands and sighed.

'OK, OK, you sit there, but you'll have to fly the plane.'

The Irishman finally came to bed at 3 in the morning. His wife asked him why he had stayed up so late.

'It's the cat's fault!' he said.

'Why?' asked his wife.

'I was waiting for him to come in,' yawned the Irishman, 'so I could put him out for the night.'

An Irishman was talking to an American in a Dublin bar about his forthcoming summer holiday to the States.

'So where are you staying?'

'I'm thinking of San Josay,' said the Irishman.

The American laughed. 'That's pronounced San Hosay. In California we pronounce 'J' as 'H'.'

'Oh thanks,' said the Irishman. 'I didn't know that.'

'No problem. So when are you going?'

'Hune and Huly,' replied the Irishman.

Pat was walking past Paddy's house when he saw a sign that read 'Boat for Sale'. Paddy was in the garden at the time.

'What's this sign all about Paddy? You haven't got a boat—all you've got out here is a old lawnmower and a garden bench!'

'I know,' said Paddy, 'and they're boat for sale.'

A drunk wobbles in to the pub and sees another man sitting at the bar.

'Can I buy you a drink?' says the drunk.

'Sure, that'll be great,' the man replies in an Irish accent.

'Hey, are you from Ireland?' asks the drunk as he gives the man his drink.

'And proud of it,' the man smiles.
The drunk responds. 'I'm from Ireland too! Let's have another drink for Ireland.' So they have another round.

'So what part of Ireland are you from?'

'County Mayo.'

'No?!' exclaims the drunk. 'I'm from County Mayo too.'

'Let's drink to County Mayo,' says the Irishman.

'What school did you go to?' slurred the drunk.

'St Mary's. I left in 1977.'
The drunk sputtered into his beer. 'I went to St Mary's and I left in 1977!'

'Another round please, barman.'
As the barman pulled their next round a regular came into the pub. 'What's happening?'

'Not much,' sighed the barman, 'apart from the Flynn twins getting drunk again.'

'Haven't seen you in here for a while,' Paddy said to Thaddy when he turned up for a drink in his local pub.

'I know,' said Thaddy. 'I've had to stay at home with the missus because of the abusive phone calls.'

'Oh I'm sorry mate. It's not nice when that happens,' sympathised Paddy.

'It's OK now. She's promised not to make any more.'

Dolan was a fanatical supporter of Ireland's worst football team, Shamrock United Rovers Athletic. At one match a man next to him started talking to him.

'Are you going to stay to the end?'

'Of course!' said Dolan.

'Here's the keys then. Lock up on your way out.'

171

An Irishman has a great party trick. He holds up his two thumbs and gets someone to choose one. When they have, he puts both his hands behind his back for a moment and then holds out his clenched fists.

'OK, which hand?'

Shamus was puzzled by something in the newspaper.

'Paddy, it says here that 8 of 10 men use ball point pens to write with.'

'So?' said Paddy.

'Well,' asked a curious Shamus, 'what do the other two use them for?'

How can you tell if you've brought an Irish ladder?

It has a sign at the top that reads 'Stop'!

A driver ran into a small train station outside Cork looking for the station-master.

'Excuse me,' he gasped, 'it's your level crossing. One of the barriers is up and the other one is down. Is everything OK?'

'Ah now, don't be worrying yourself,' said the station-master, 'we're half expecting a train.'

Paddy was telling Pat about a disturbing sight from the previous night.

'Oh it was horrible, Pat,' Paddy said. 'It had 32 legs, 32 arms, 12 teeth and was all wrinkled and smelled like a vapour rub.'

'Bejabers Paddy, what was it? Some kind of monster?'

'No,' replied Pat. 'The front row of a Val Doonican tribute concert.'

A young Irish lad was talking to his fiancée.

'I want to marry an intelligent woman, a good woman, and a woman who will make me happy.'

'Will you please make up your mind?'

An Irish girl rang the doctor in a panic one morning.

'Doctor, I've just woken up and I've got a pimple on the side of my face.'

'So?' replied the doctor. 'Most people have pimples on the side of their faces at some time.'

'But this one has a tiny tree growing from it!' said the Irish girl. 'And under the tree is a little pond and next to that is a tiny set of chairs and a table with a picnic laid out on it.'

'Oh there's nothing to worry about,' said the doctor. 'It's just a beauty spot.'

A man went into a Dublin bank and asked the cashier if she could check his balance.

'Certainly, Sir,' said the Irish cashier. She got up, walked around to the man's side of the counter and pushed him over.

An American and an Irish tourist were looking at the Niagara Falls.

'Will you look at that. What a sight! I bet you don't have anything like that in Ireland?'

'We don't,' said the Irishman. 'But we've got plumbers who could fix it.'

Two Irish girls were discussing what to get their friend for her birthday.

'What about a book?' suggested one of them.

'No,' said her friend. 'She's already got one of those and she hasn't coloured it in yet!'

Imagine the Christmas story if the Three Wise Men had been Three Irish Mothers.

They wouldn't have had to ask for directions, they would have arrived on time, helped deliver the baby, cleaned up the stable, made a nice Irish stew and brought practical presents.

'I helped my husband become a millionaire,' the Irish girl boasted.

'Really,' said her friend. 'And what was he before?'

'A billionaire,' sighed the Irish girl.

An ageing Irish playboy sidles up to a pretty young girl at a party.

'I say gorgeous, where have you been all my life?'

The young girl looked at him, disgusted.

'Well, for most of it, I wasn't born.'

Two Irish tramps were paddling in the sea when one of them looked down at the other's feet.

'Bejabers. Your feet are filthy.'

'I know,' said the second Irish tramp. 'We didn't come here last year.'

An Irishman went for a job. The interviewer asked him his name.

'Oh now, that's a difficult one. I've to think about that one.'

'Concentrate,' said the interviewer.

'No, it's longer than that!' replied the Irishman.

Now I'm not saying that Titch O'Malley was the smallest man in Ireland, but he was late for work the other day because he was cleaning out the budgie's cage and the door slammed shut.

An Irishman was hitchhiking along a road when a big black hearse stopped beside him. The driver offered him a lift.

'No thanks,' said the Irishman. 'I wasn't thinking of going that far!'

The Wicklow fire brigade had just received a brand new fire engine.

'So what are we going to do with the old engine?' asked one of the fire fighters. 'Are we going to dump it?'

'No we're not,' said the Station chief. 'We'll use the old one for false alarms.'

You don't see too many Irish snowmen around, do you?

That's because they take longer to build—you have to spend time hollowing the head out!

Did you hear the one about the Irish wife who showed her husband a picture of a very expensive outfit in a catalogue?

She told him that she would really like it, so the Irish husband cut it out and gave it to her!

'I'm sorry,' said the doctor. 'There's not a lot I can do for you. You are suffering from alcoholic constipation.'

'What do you mean, doc?' asked the Irishman. 'Is that serious?'

'You find it almost impossible to pass a pub.'

A young lad went into a joke shop in Dublin and asked the owner for some invisible ink.

'Certainly!' said the owner. 'What colour?'

Another Drop of Irish Jokes

Did you hear the one about the Irishwoman who flew all the way to Alaska to make her dinner?

She bought a ready meal whose instructions read, 'Prepare from a frozen state'!

Did you hear the one about the Irish inventor who crossed an electric blanket with a toaster?

It worked really well but he kept popping out of bed at night!

Did you hear the one about the Irish lighthouse keeper who bought a corner unit?

When he got it home he couldn't find anywhere to put it!

Paddy O'Paddy died and as he was a sailor all his life, requested that he be buried at sea. Unfortunately three Irish gravediggers died digging his grave.

Did you hear the one about the Irishwoman who went out with her purse open?

She heard on the radio that there was a chance of some change in the weather!

An Irishman went into his local library and slammed a book down on the counter.

'This book I borrowed last week was absolute rubbish. It had far too many characters, very little in the way of dialogue and absolutely no plot whatsoever.'

'Is that right?' said the Librarian. 'So you were the person who took our phone book!'

Did you hear the one about the Irishwoman who would buy anything that was marked down?

She went out the other Saturday and bought three dresses and an escalator!

Scientists in Germany have crossed a popular festive bird with an Irishman and got a turkey that looks forward to Christmas.

It was an Irishman's first day on a Dublin building site and he climbed up a very tall ladder, but when he got to the top he felt very dizzy.

'Oh I don't feel too well!' he called down to the foreman.

'Well come on down then,' said the foreman.

'How will I get down?' asked the Irishman.

'The same way you got up.'

'Oh I won't be doing that,' said the Irishman.

'Why not?' shouted the foreman.

'I came up head first.'

An Englishman, a Scotsman and an Irishman were stopped on High Street by the police and asked for their names. Not wishing to give their real names the Englishman looked about and then said 'John Sainsburys.' The Scotsman looked around and said 'Mark Spencer.' The Irishman did the same and said 'Bradford and Bingley Building Society.'

Did you hear about the young Irish girl who was convinced that the programme 'Pop Idol ' was a show about lazy dads?

Pat and Paddy were lying in bed together. Pat looked at Paddy and Paddy looked at Pat and Pat said,

'I don't think much of this wife swapping, do you?'

Did you hear the one about the Irishman who bought skis?

Unfortunately he was very badly injured when he tried to slalom down a waterfall!

'Have you heard my new knock-knock joke?' asked Paddy.

'No I haven't,' answers Thaddy.

'Great,' says Paddy. 'You start.'

Did you hear the one about the Irishman who won the Dublin Marathon in record time?

He was asked to do a lap of honour!

An Irishman walks into a bar sporting a big black eye.

'Who gave you that?' asked the barman.

'Nobody gave it to me,' said the Irishman. 'I had to fight for it.'

Did you hear the one about Ireland's smallest builder?

His first ever job was on a building site for Lego!

An Irishman was dead against fox hunting so he decided to be a hunt saboteur.

He found out when the next local hunt was, went out the night before and shot the fox.

Did you hear the tale of the poor unfortunate Irishwoman who fell out of her window?

She was trying to iron her curtains!

'So Paddy, how long have you believed in reincarnation?' Thaddy asked Paddy.
'Ever since I was a little frog.'

Two Irish cannibals are eating a clown. One says to the other:

'Does this taste funny to you?'

Three Irishmen went ice fishing but didn't catch a thing. By the time they cut a hole big enough for their boat, it was time to go home.

How do you make an Irish person laugh on a Sunday?

Tell them a joke on a Friday night!

The boss looked over the shoulder of his new Irish secretary.

'Your typing has really improved. I can only see five mistakes. Well done! Now type the second word.'

An American tourist was visiting Ireland when he stopped outside O'Toole's farm for a chat.

'Nice farm, buddy,' he says. 'I got one at home in Texas. It takes me nearly six hours to drive all around it.'

'Is that right Sir? I've got a tractor like that too.'

An Irishman rang up his nearest cinema.

'Is that the local cinema?'

'Well now, that would depend on where you're calling from.'

An Irishman wasn't feeling very well so he went to see his doctor, Dr Will C. U. Nye, for a check up. After some tests the doctor returned with the results and by the look on his face, it wasn't good news.

'I'm afraid I have some very bad news,' says the doctor. 'You are dying and you don't have long to live.'

Naturally the Irishman was distraught. 'Oh Doctor, how long have I got left?'

'Ten...' the doctor replies in a somewhat solemn tone.

'Ten?' cries the Irishman. 'Ten what? Years? Months? How long have I got left?'

The doctor answers, 'Nine, eight, seven...'

An Irishwoman found her husband standing in front of a mirror with his eyes closed.

'What you doing?' asked the Irishwoman.

'Trying to see what I look like asleep,' said the Irishman.